EDUCATION REIMAGINED

Changes Required in the U.S. Education System from Students' Perspectives

EDUCATION REIMAGINED

Changes Required in the U.S. Education System from Students' Perspectives

Maruf Hossain

Copyright © 2021 Maruf Hossain.

All rights reserved. No part of this book may be reproduced in any form or by any electronic or mechanical means, including information storage and retrieval systems, without permission in writing from the publisher, except by reviewers, who may quote brief passages in a review.

ISBN: 978-1-956074-16-1 (Paperback Edition)
ISBN: 978-1-956074-17-8 (Hardcover Edition)
ISBN: 978-1-956074-15-4 (E-book Edition)

Book Ordering Information

Phone Number: 315 288-7939 ext. 1000 or 347-901-4920
Email: info@globalsummithouse.com
Global Summit House
www.globalsummithouse.com

Printed in the United States of America

Contents

Preface

Acknowledgements

Part I: The Reality of the Education System

1. Standardized Testing

2. The Bullying Epidemic

3. Families and a Student's Education

4. Learning with Disabilities

5. The Administration

6. The Price of Our Education

7. Preparing and Transitioning to College

8. The College Experience

9. Customized Education

10. The Future of the US Education System

Part II: Voices of the System

1. Education's Purpose by Corrina Blau

2. A Diversified Approach to American Education by Raimondo Graziano

3. Civics in Education: An American Approach by Raimondo Graziano

4. Cut the Middle Man: Why Current High School Education Is Irrelevant by Scott Fleisher

5. Mental Health of the Future by Urooj Ansari

6. Discrimination Experienced by Students in the Education System by Nayema Laboni

7. Freedom to Teach by Joy Lam

8. Institutionalize Mandated Diversity by Yelena Dzhanova

9. Student's Education Institution Transition by Maruf Hossain

Contributors

Bibliography

About the Author

Preface

The United States has always been the land of opportunity and equal rights. One of the biggest things that it is known for, especially by foreigners, is the U.S. education system—unless, of course, you study education systems around the world and compare it with the United States. For those that go through the US education system from the start in kindergarten to the end of college, we've seen and experienced the system and seen firsthand how everything plays out. Everyone's experience is different. However, everyone can agree upon some of the major issues students face in the US education system. The United States government controls much of how the education system runs and how things should be. However, many students, parents, teachers, and education advocates have voiced their issues and concerns, and they go unheard and unchanged because the government refuses to change the system.

Therefore, people who study the education system and follow what will compare the US education system with many of the education systems in Europe. We have come to a point in our education system where we understand that the students have become the government, and the government has become the students. The government may be in power, but they are not making major nationwide changes to benefit the students of the system. Through this understanding, this book was written to give students a voice to speak up and speak out against the education system and to bring into light some of the major issues in the US education system along with creative ideas and solutions from those that have contributed and volunteered to write for the book along with me, and education advocate.

The contributors of this book were gathered through social media advertising and word of mouth multiple times. At first, many wanted to write for the book, but many of them also dropped out of their own will. Through this effort, I was left with the contributors that wrote a narrative for the book, along with my narrative. For the narratives, the contributors were asked to choose a topic or issue that they wanted to see a change for in the US education system. Furthermore, they were asked to share their personal story if they had any regarding the topic and how it affected them, and their experience with the topic. Afterward, they were told to explain the change required in the system regarding their topic of choice. Lastly, they were asked to talk about the future of the system in a general matter, if possible, and the future of the US education system with and without their proposal for change.

We can no longer follow a corrupt education system that does not work for the students of our great nation. The ultimate hope is that the federal and state government, the board of education, teachers, parents, students, and others who oversee our schools and colleges worldwide read this book and understand where we, as students, come from. The book targets the students and parents who are victims of the education system and the lawmakers who oversee the education system and make nationwide changes to better the students in the system. There must be an understanding of the victim we have become and how invaluable our education system has become. Furthermore, through that understanding, the changes we ask for and require to be tested out and implemented. We are truly at a time with our education system where the students have become the government, and the government has become the students.

Acknowledgments

I want to acknowledge the contributors who have volunteered to write for part 2 of the book. Without their contribution, this book would not be as valuable as it is. This shows that students can come together to speak up and speak out to make a change for the future of our country and, more importantly, the future generations of the US education system. We can now only hope and move this cause forward to the best of our ability to get the government to hear us and make the changes we ask for as a starting point and get others to voice their opinions and see the changes we hope to see blossom and be effective for students of the United States's education system.

Thank you to Corrina Blau, Raimondo Graziano, Scott Fleisher, Urooj Ansari, Nayema Laboni, Joy Lam, and Yelena Dzhanova. Without all of you, this book would not have come to be. Thank you for volunteering, taking time out of your busy schedule to write narratives for this book, and looking at the bigger picture and cause for this book. Thank you for speaking up and speaking out against the US education system and giving insightful information on some of the major issues of the education system and expressing what many of you have personally gone through. I am amazed by reading so many of your stories, not just because of your stories but also because you expressed your concern for the issue you wished to write and your writing style. I think these forms of voices are required to see the changes we hope the government makes. We can no longer follow a corrupt education system that does not work for the students of our great nation. It's time we see change.

Part I

The Reality of the Education System

Standardized Testing

The United States' education system has become infamous for standardized testing. The most infamous concept of how a student is evaluated is through testing, which consists of in-class quizzes, tests, and major exams, along with the end-of-year state exams. *Standardized tests* are tests that are supposed to determine how well a student knows the material given in the test. These tests play a major role in determining how well students know the subject on certain topics every few weeks. Major tests at the end of the year determine if the student will pass the class or grade and move on to the next grade. Testing is introduced to children as young as five when they are in kindergarten. From there, these students are put through rigorous exams and quizzes while being taught what is asked of by the state and the local board of education rather than having a choice of what to learn. These tests have evolved into a key issue in the US education system that devalues a child's intelligence and comprehension of information taught in class.

The history of standardized testing began in 1838 when American educators began articulating the formal assessment of a student's achievement.[1] From there followed the creation

---

[1] "History of Standardized Testing in the United States," NEA History of Standardized

of some of the major standardized tests we know today, such as the Scholastic Aptitude Test (SAT) that started in 1926[2] and the American College Testing Program (ACT) that started in 1959.[3] Other tests such as SHSAT, Regents, and the citywide state tests students take at the end of the school year in elementary and middle school. If we are to evaluate the purpose of a test and why the US education system has chosen testing to be the end-all and be-all of student assessment, we can secretly see it for its own agenda.

The US Congress Office of Technology Assessment describes the purpose of testing as the assessment of student learning, school accountability, and educational opportunities for students.[4] However, testing as an assessment of student learning only shows a certain percentage of what the student may know regarding the test. What it does not show is their full understanding and full potential on the topics or the subject. At the end of the day, you should realize that schools, colleges, universities, and other educational institutions are funded by the state government in some way, but for them to be funded, they also have to submit statistical information on the performance of the entire school. Therefore, the only way they would be able to do that is through giving tests and using student quantitative data from testing and hiring a statistician to evaluate the school's performance based on student's grades that will be submitted to the government for future funding. Schools that do not do well or have a bad rep have a chance of shutting down unless it can

---

Testing, 2002, accessed November 24, 2016, http://www.nea.org/home/66139.htm.
2 Ibid.
3 "Annual Report 2015," 2015 ACT Annual Report, 2015, accessed November 24, 2016, http://www.act.org/content/dam/act/unsecured/documents/AnnualReport2015.pdf.
4 "Testing in American Schools: Asking the Right Question," Testing in American Schools: Asking the Right Question, February 1992, accessed November 24, 2016, https://www.princeton.edu/~ota/disk1/1992/9236/9236.PDF

improve. That is generally how the US education system is run.

Nonetheless, all the testing and studying a student does only go so far during the actual testing. It does not take a psychologist or a psychology student to realize the strain testing can put on a child. We know some of the more common things are test anxiety, procrastination, over evaluating a test or a situation, all-nighters before exams, etc... These are only some of the psychological effects testing can have on a student, and it does not do any good to the student's mental health and well-being. With testing, you are ultimately saying that a student is somehow supposed to understand, conceptualize, and internalize information well enough on not just one but multiple topics to do at least satisfactory work to maintain a good GPA. The reality of how students are and how studying is for them is a completely different story. Students do not choose what to focus on and when they are all given multiple homework and assignments outside of the studying, they all have to focus on. The education system has chosen testing as a way to take over the lives of students.

There has to be a way for a child to be balanced in life between home, schooling, religious duties, extracurricular activities, social activities, and downtime on a daily and weekly basis. From age five, students go through this process of waking up for school, going to school, coming home, doing homework, studying, and then going to sleep, only to repeat the process. From K to 12, that is usually the case, aside from extracurricular activities and social time they may have allotted to within their day. Nevertheless, with everything they go through, schooling and testing take up most of their day, let alone their lives. While education is important and a priority, it should not be something that seems more of a job than the enjoyment of learning and getting educated. The education system takes the fun out of learning due to its rigorous standards and testing a student. The balance of home life, schooling, religious duties, extracurricular activities, social activities, and downtime on a daily and weekly basis. From age five, students go through this process of waking up for school, going to school, coming home, doing homework, studying, and then going to sleep, only to repeat the process. From K to 12, that is usually the case, aside from extracurricular activities and social time they may have allotted to within their day. Nevertheless, with everything they go through, schooling and testing take up most of their day, let alone their lives. While education is important and a priority, it should not be something that seems more of a job than the enjoyment of learning and getting educated. The education system takes the fun out of learning due to its rigorous standards and testing a student. The balance of home life, schooling, religious duties, extracurricular activities, social activities, and downtime needs to be met instead of what students face today. Students are forced into this schooling and testing system that takes up their lives rather than coming up with a new way to balance everything I just mentioned.

    In the twenty-first century, testing students have become infamous among students, parents, and education advocates that we now see protests and movements to stop standardized testing. Testing only tells us a small percentage of what a student may know by the time the test day comes. Before giving these tests, we never think about how much capability each specific student does have in studying for a test—their test-taking skills, studying skills, domestic situation, personal issues, etc... These are crucial things to think about if we are grading students on a test because factors like these have a major impact on how well students may do during the test. A test does not give us a complete picture or potential students may have in relaying the knowledge gained from the class. They study but are then limited to how much knowledge they have by the time of the test, and then using that limited knowledge, they take a test. Students should not be graded or evaluated in such a way. There is a calling and a need for change in how we evaluate our kids in a classroom and then, overall, their subject performance through these standardized tests.

If we should not evaluate our students through testing, what can we do to evaluate their school performance? The way to assess their learning goes back to performance assessment through the portfolio-based education system popular in the 1980s and 1990s. While due to its setbacks, it has been discontinued, a proper, well-structured, and thought-out way of implementing the system is required more than ever if we are to take away the testing system finally. The main concern with the portfolios seems to be the design and execution of the system, the creation, maintenance, and assessment, and its time consumption.[5] These issues need to be reevaluated, and the portfolio system needs to be recreated for better results and less stress. The main issue with the portfolio-based education system is the teacher or professor's time consumption to create enough work to be evaluated throughout the year. If we are to bulk on the number of things a student gets graded on, it can be overwhelming. Therefore, a reformatted portfolio system needs to be created, so it is fair for all forms of students and less strain on the teachers/professors.

A portfolio is a set of work that is self-analyzed in a set

---

5 "Portfolio Definition," Entry, May 15, 2013, accessed November 24, 2016, http://edglossary.org/portfolio/.

period cumulated as a record of achievement.[6] A few things need to happen for a portfolio system to work in a classroom setting to assess students. Students should not be overwhelmed with the amount of work given to them throughout the year. A proposal for the portfolio-based education system to be implemented in the US education system is the following: teachers and professors need to plan out the school year or the semester assignments. Rather than overwhelming oneself as the teacher with the work by the students, plan out the number of assignments to be assigned. Each assignment should be given back to the students several times with notes to improve their work before giving a final grade that will count toward the marking period or the semester. A classic rule that can be followed is three strikes, and you are out. That would mean each student gets three chances at each assignment to continuously improve their work to make sure they get that A+ and have an equal opportunity to succeed at their work.

Furthermore, different forms of assessment should include the following: short written assignments that are done in class; larger assignments for the home, such as a term paper given to students to work on for a few weeks, whatever the teacher feels fit; and for older students in high school and college, class presentations. All the assignments should be allotted enough time for students to research the topic, study the topic at their own time, and create a presentation or complete the assignment or paper given. For all forms of assignments other than the presentations, students should get a total of three chances to improve their work before they hand in the final product,

---

6 "Performance Assessment in an Era of Standards-Based Educational Accountability," Stanford Center for Opportunity Policy in Education, 2010, accessed November 24, 2016, https://scale.stanford.edu/system/files/performance-assessment-era-standards-based-educational-accountability.pdf.

which is graded and counted toward the end of the marking period or semester. With the presentations, they should be given enough time, and it should be during major times of the school year like school midterms and final seasons. If students are given at least a month, they can study the subject and create a proper presentation.

This form of portfolio system should be tested, and the response seen by the students and teachers alike. Through this portfolio system, students have more time and flexibility in how to spend their day, how to use their time wisely to do their assignments and not be overwhelmed or stressed about the upcoming test, or how to get all the topics and information they were taught in a set period into their brain. It is also a stress reliever that they faced in the 1980s and 1990s, as I can imagine for teachers. Through this system, assignments and graded materials are further spread out, and a manageable amount of work is given to students throughout the school year. This way, the students are happy, but parents and teachers can also be more relaxed with the work given. Furthermore, more time on each topic can be spent during class time, so the students get more time on each topic and are well versed on the topic, rather than moving topic to topic each week only to be tested every few weeks. Testing, for it to be a means to assess knowledge on a topic, has led to friction and a backlash from education advocates, parents, and students. Our teachers teach us things that are specifically instructed by the local board of education or the state government. While they are taught, the implications and full equality of understanding, comprehending, and internalizing the information given are in question. No students are alike, and we do not know how well each student truly understands, comprehends, and internalizes the information taught in class. Rather they are required to learn everything being taught, go back home to review, or be tutored on the same material one-on-one again to get a clearer or better understanding of the material taught in class. Afterward, a test is given once the topic or topics are taught in a set time, only to gather statistical data for the school's funding. These tests that people are revolting against are not in favor of the students and their learning. However, they are the ones being most affected by the standardized testing system.

    Another issue with testing to assess a student's understanding of a topic or multiple topics is the amount of time spent on the topic before moving on to a new one. Teachers must cover a set number of topics on the subject for the year or the semester. Therefore, a number of these topics are covered in a short period. It may be that a teacher covers a few in a set number of weeks and then gives a test on those. The problem here is that the student may not know several topics that are going to be covered in their test. Therefore, topics covered months ago might show up in a test while the student understands that the test would be on the current topics they are learning. Therefore, since material from the past just came out of nowhere in their test, and they did not know of it and did not review the material, they might not have done well. There are two issues in this situation. One is that there is a miscommunication between students and the teachers, and number two, a student does not get to study for all the materials on the test and has a negative grade due to it. This is aside from anyone knowing if the student is even prepared or has conceptualized anything from the past since the class continues moving on with the topics.

    In classes, there is always an exception or two of students that struggle more than their peers, and while they do should not receive any special treatment unless there is something specific medically that is known to give, such as extra time on a test, we may not know the full extent of their struggles in their studies. Therefore, with the class moving on, we leave these kids behind that are having an extra hard time than the rest of their peers in their class.

Even if a teacher knows a student does not do well or has an extra hard time in the subject, there is not much anyone, let alone a teacher, who can help the child. Sometimes, all the students are getting tutoring service in their school or private tutoring outside their school. However, they are the type of students that are suffering the most due to tests. All teachers can move from topic to topic at their own time to make sure they cover all the material mandated by the board of education or the state. There is no equality of success in teaching and learning for all forms of students. Everyone is stuck in a corrupt system of student assessment that is not fair and does not work.

There are many psychological effects on students that deprive them personally, socially, and mentally. It is not that they do not have an equal opportunity at education, but they do not have an equal opportunity at educational success due highly to the testing system. Personally and mentally, for a student, testing impacts their mindset and their self-esteem. Testing can be intimidating to face, especially when a child knows he cannot provide satisfactory work or seem to not improve in tests and class. Testing can then play mind games with the child, and his faith in his abilities may go astray. From a social standpoint, a child may be criticized by his/her peers for his/her performance in tests or school generally. There are social impacts such as being called a nerd or the pressure of doing well and maintaining a certain grade at all times from parents and family members.

These are all negative forces acting against children to do well and stressing them in many ways. The biggest issue in all of this is that they do not have a second chance in tests. Whatever they receive in their tests is what they have to accept. There is no redo or extra time to improve in their work. Lastly, it impacts their GPA when they get their report card or their transcript.

A reimagined-portfolio education system needs to be thought of, taught, and implemented in the US education system. We should be willing to change the way we measure a student's success. The fight against stopping standardized testing has been going on for years. What I proposed is stopping standardized testing from adopting the portfolio-based education system. However, before the portfolio education system is implemented, proper execution and teaching methods should be thought of and researched. Nevertheless, I proposed that giving students three chances and how assignments should be spread out would be the best of worlds for both the educators and the students. Until, as a nation, we choose to stop the testing system and find a new way to measure the success of a student, this education system will always have an excuse by the students and an asterisk next to the name.

Currently, the US education system is dependent on schooling children and testing their intelligence of the materials taught through standardized testing. This can become overwhelming for students, if not at a young age, definitely in their later years of schooling. We may see this system as a form of stress or anxiety, and eventually maybe even lack effort in school studies from the students due to the number of tests and the strain it takes on them. In the later years of schooling (such as in high school and definitely college), students may be required to take more than one test in one day and multiple tests in a week. This is most relevant during midterms and finals. Teachers put all this pressure on multiple topics for these tests and expect all students to be somehow able to study for all this. Instead, we see students going crazy studying for these tests, having all-nighters, drinking coffee and energy drinks, and consuming caffeine all day to get through their day and the night, only to be restless and unfocused or barely ready when it is time to take the test. These are the types of issues we face as a reality of the testing system. We, as a nation, starting with the government, need to implement proper grading standards to replace the testing system.

The change we need to see in the American education system has to start on a federal level, from Congress and the president. While the US education system is governed through the state government, I have emphasized this education change and am calling for a federal change. The portfolio-based education system needs to be properly reevaluated and recreated for the equal success of all students. This change has to occur in all fifty states, not just a few that understand the issue of the testing system and pass a bill to stop the testing system. Without the change and not adhering to the voices of education advocates, students, and parents, we remain ignorant as a nation to a major issue that asks for change but, not much has been done.

Standardized testing has been one of the forefront issues in the US education system in the twenty-first century. By retaining things as they are with standardized testing, students will not reach their full potential, and it will always be just a competition in the job market. If all students can truly have an equal chance at acing their classes, the competition in the job market will no longer rely on a student's grades in school, and even if it does, the true potential of a student will still be shown. A student's GPA does not even play a big factor anymore, and it is more of their past experiences and knowledge that relies on their job. However, some jobs do have specific requirements as far as grades are concerned.

Furthermore, their true knowledge of the job they are pursuing would be due to their job skills and knowledge on the subject. The value of the US education system has been in question throughout the twenty-first century, and a calling to end standardized testing has been voiced. Standardized testing has been one of the top issues being voiced to stop by the public because, by now, most people see the value of knowledge a test has on a student and their future. However, aside from a few exceptional states, the federal or state governments have not done anything to end standardized testing. In the US education system, standardized testing is one of the top issues that negatively affect students and gives the US education system a bad name. Everyone in America may have the right to an education, but they do not have an equal opportunity to succeed in the American education system.

The Bullying Epidemic

The issue of bullying is an epidemic faced by kids of our society today, and it has become one of the top issues, if not the biggest issue in our education system. Bullying is the unwanted violence between two individuals that may be physical, verbal, or cyber. In a bullying situation, multiple individuals play a role in its prevention. Nevertheless, the individuals involved are the perpetrators, victims, bystanders, school officials, and the parents of both the perpetrator and victim. Everyone has a crucial, role in its prevention. With how bullying has become a movement over the past few years and with the awareness of bullying on the rise, there are many ways to prevent bullying, and it all starts with getting educated about bullying and how to prevent it. Bullying is an epidemic that may not be completely stopped. There may never be a day where we hear there is no bullying whatsoever. However, we have all the responsibility to prevent it.

In a bullying situation, a perpetrator is an individual that provokes an individual to react and uses different forms of violence to impact the victim. In other words, he/she is the one that uses physical violence, verbal and emotional abuse, or embarrasses or puts down an individual on the Internet.

Through schooling and growing up, we hear those perpetrators of bullying are bullying others because of their insecurities or family life. With many of these perpetrators, what we hear growing up is that they may be facing issues at home or in their personal lives. The root cause of what the individual has become and why he chooses to frustrate other individuals needs to be discovered. It is important to find out why he/she is doing what he/she is doing and why he/she has become a perpetrator of bullying. For the perpetrators of bullying, they must get educated through programs and organizations on the effects of bullying and teach them what they are doing is wrong. The only way to help him/her is to talk to the person and see how educators, programs, and organizations that work on bullying prevention help that individual. In a confidential environment, it may help get the perpetrator into counseling to see what is going on in their personal lives and help them.

A victim is an individual that is negatively affected by bullying and is going through physical, verbal, emotional, and cyberbullying. This is the innocent individual affected by bullying, usually due to no fault of his/her own. Many psychological effects can occur due to how their peers are mistreating them. Often, we see that they may be bullied because there is something about them that does not sit well with the perpetrators. There may be many reasons as to why they have become a target of bullying. It could be anywhere from the way they look or dress, them being minorities and the stigmas around them. However, this does not make the act of bullying on the victims acceptable. Bullying can lead to persons feeling that they are outcasts in their school and social settings when they are around their peers.

Depending on how the individuals get bullied, they

can face many forms of psychological issues. They may go through depression, suicidal thoughts, and post-traumatic stress disorder (PTSD), to name a few. The more extreme the violence the victim experiences, the more severe the effect will be on him. The way to help him/her is through a school's antibullying prevention program or peer mediation. Families and victims of bullying should know the antibullying school rules set in place and get psychological counseling to cope with the bullying.

Outside of being a victim or perpetrator of bullying, everyone around the two individuals has the biggest role in preventing it. The individuals involved in this aspect of bullying are bystanders, school officials, and parents. These individuals can prevent bullying and should be there to stop it and help the perpetrators and victims of bullying. Let us start with the bystanders. Bystanders of bullying are seeing someone get bullied and not doing anything to prevent bullying. As a bystander, what you are doing is promoting violence and bullying. Without any action, there is no chance that we see. The bystanders should seek help if they cannot stop the bullying themselves. Now among peers, that may or may not happen. In a school setting, there is an issue with being a snitch. Students, especially in middle and high school, do not accept students who snitch. We may see that by becoming a snitch, you also become a victim of bullying. We need to educate students and show that it is okay to tell school officials to get help and prevent bullying. You may be stopping a serious and fatal condition by getting help. By being a bystander, you are only part of the problem, and you are in no way helping the situation, let alone the innocent victim of bullying.

School officials and parents are at the core of stopping bullying. Bullying mainly occurs in school settings. Therefore, the teachers, security guards, deans, and other administrative faculty and staff have the biggest role to be on the lookout to prevent bullying. From time to time, what we may see are victims getting bullied by their school peers and getting bullied by their teachers. That is another issue on its own. Teachers and other school officials should not in any way be the perpetrator of bullying. However, if they are, I think it is safe to say they are not fit to be educators or be in a school setting, and the principal should take proper actions to deal with such individuals.

Nevertheless, parents and educators should implement proper education on students to prevent bullying. In a school setting, there should be antibullying rules and prevention. The education system and antibullying organizations should train educators on what to implement as an antibullying rule in the school and prevent bullying. We also have to follow up on it and make sure educators are properly enforcing the antibullying rules or laws for their school.

Furthermore, the core to bullying prevention starts at home with the parents and the kids. Parents are required to teach their kids the causes and effects of bullying and always lead by example. As parents, they may be the reason a person is a perpetrator of bullying. This goes back to reasons why a perpetrator may become a bully, and a lot of the time, we hear that it may be because of their domestic environment. First and foremost, if it is due to domestic situations, it is highly important to get help, and it starts with getting educated and learning how to help the perpetrator. I talk more about this in detail in the next chapter. For the parents of the victims and perpetrators of bullying, I think getting the message out to their children on bullying is highly crucial, and implementing the right principles in raising the child is how we can help prevent someone from becoming a bully being a victim. If there are antibullying programs in the local community or in the school, the children and the parents need to be actively involved.

With the bullying epidemic, there are multiple statistics of bullying gathered by antibullying governmental organizations and other programs. We should be alerted and be there to look out for victims of bullying, especially with statistics like "over 3.2 million students are victims of bullying each year."[7] There are many other effects of bullying for those that experience it. The students may even drop out of school because of bullying. It takes such a toll on the students that sometimes it is too much for the children to bear and so they drop out or something worse may happen. The worst thing that we may see is teachers who see nothing wrong in bullying or respond to bullying poorly.[8] These are only some of the statistics of bullying, and it is our job to prevent these from happening and bettering our schools and the education system. Recently, over the past fifteen years, another major issue with bullying we have seen on the rise involves minority groups. More specifically, Muslim students are targets of bullying.

The issue of targeted groups being bullied has been on the rise since the 9/11 bombing of the twin towers, more so than ever. Every now and then, we hear minority groups facing different forms of bullying, and with what we hear about in the news, it can feel like it is more than bullying. What we are facing in the United States today is that minority groups—not just Muslims but multiple minority groups—are facing bullying.[9] There is a

---

7 "11 Facts about Bullying," accessed November 25, 2016, https://www.dosomething.org/us/facts/11-facts-about-bullying.
8 Ibid
9 Omar Sacirby, "Muslim Teens Push Back Against 9/11 Bullying," *Huffington Post* (The Huffington Post), September 8, 2011, http://www.huffingtonpost.com/2011/09/07/

fine line between bullying and discriminating, racial profiling, and stereotyping minorities. This is an issue that I feel needs to have its terminology and to be defined as such. This form of bullying is what I call *racial and stereotyped bullying*.

Racial and stereotyped bullying. *Discriminating, labeling, and using different forms of violence on minority groups in school and social settings due to their race, religion, culture, sex, and stereotypical beliefs. Violence faced by minority groups may be physical, verbal, or emotional.*

Muslim students face this issue of racial and stereotyped bullying due to the events of 9/11. The problem here and with any form of terror attacks in our country by a Muslim name is that once a Muslim name is given in the media about the attack, it is believed all Muslims are as such. However, what people are not educated upon is that not all Muslims promote violence of any kind, let alone terror attacks on innocent lives, because it is not up to us as human beings to determine the life and death of others, and it is also not part of the teachings in Islam. It is issues like this that make us Muslim students the victim of bullying ever since 9/11.[10]

While there may be policies put in place for bullying in school settings, there are no federal laws against bullying in the United States.[11] Federal law needs to be created for the benefit of everyone in a school setting. In many ways, it has not been until recently, over the past decade, that there has been an emphasis on the issue of bullying. In many ways, the issue of bullying has been overlooked until now. Therefore, antibullying laws

---

bullying-muslim-teens-push-back_n_952947.html.
10 Omar Sacirby, "Muslim Teens Push Back Against 9/11 Bullying," *Huffington Post* (The Huffington Post), September 8, 2011, http://www.huffingtonpost.com/2011/09/07/bullying-muslim-teens-push-back_n_952947.html.
11 Federal Laws," StopBullying.gov, March 8, 2012, accessed November 25, 2016, https://www.stopbullying.gov/laws/federal/index.html.

and school prevention policies need to be made and enforced. Without a federal law, we are leaving our kids to suffer in the end. We need to be the change-makers of our generation and make bullying a priority, and we need to do everything we can to prevent bullying if we cannot stop it forever.

Even though we may not have federal laws put in place for bullying, there are civil rights laws through the Department of Education and Department of Justice that must be enforced and implemented.[12] These are laws that should be carefully reviewed and, if needed, should be reported to the Department of Justice and Department of Education, especially if your school administration does not take the proper measures. If students face racial and stereotyped bullying and nothing is being done about it, and if something extreme occurs, then the incident should be reported to the Department of Justice. Extreme in this case would be something such as a Muslim student being called a terrorist and rumors are being made about the student. Some things cannot be overlooked, and extreme measures should be taken before it is too late. Imagine students being called terrorists and false rumors such as a Muslim student blowing up their school being said about someone. It is those kinds of situations where students and parents need to report to the school and see what they will do and report to the Department of Justice and the board of education.

Parents and students should look over and get familiar with the Department of Justice's website and look at all the educational opportunities and discrimination laws available for them. There are discriminatory laws to protect students from racial and national origin discrimination, sex-based discrimination, religious discrimination, and disability discrimination laws.[13]

---

12 Ibid.
13 "Types of Educational Opportunities Discrimination," Justice.gov, August 7,

If students face bullying or discrimination to such extremes, where it now falls into any of the laws of the Department of Justice, they should get in contact with the civil rights division of the Department of Justice. An example of this reporting with the example of the student being accused of being a terrorist would be religious discrimination. In this case, the parent and the student can file religious discrimination under Title IV of the Civil Rights Act of 1964. With such a reporting, a person can address discrimination and harassment based on religion and spans all religious affiliations.[14] The first step would be to report bullying and discrimination to school officials and find out or see what school officials will do to end racial and stereotypical bullying. If nothing is being done to bring justice on such an issue, then reporting it to the Department of Justice civil rights division would be the place to go.

Parents and students can also report these forms of bullying turned discrimination through the US Department of Education and the Office for Civil Rights[15] that inform us of the various forms of discrimination in school settings. When we see or hear these forms of discrimination, we usually immediately picture discrimination by the school. However, our society has only worsened to where many of these forms of discrimination are among peers, which only call it bullying. These forms of bullying, which I termed and defined as racial and stereotyped bullying, are forms of discrimination among peers in school settings. It is minorities that go through these forms of discrimination, whether it be race and national origin discrimination or something else. Those that face these

---

2015, accessed November 26, 2016, https://www.justice.gov/crt/types-educational-opportunities-discrimination.
14 Ibid.
15 "US Department of Education," Office for Civil Rights, May 4, 2015, accessed November 29, 2016, http://www2.ed.gov/about/offices/list/ocr/index.html.

discriminations can report it to the Office for Civil Rights through their online form, mail, or e-mail promptly of 180 days since the incident.[16]

With the federal protections students and parents have with the US Department of Justice and the Office for Civil Rights, there is a set procedure of reporting through these resources. Since some of the bullied students go through may seem discrimination or racial and stereotyped bullying, these forms of bullying and discrimination should be reported to these resources if the school officials do not take the proper measures depending on the extreme length of the bullying or discrimination. Parents and students that have to report these should follow a chain of command of reporting as follows:

1. Report to school officials (guidance counselor, dean, principal, etc…) to take the proper steps required by the Office for Civil Rights and the US Department of Justice.

2. If the proper steps are not taken promptly and/or no action is taken to justify the situation and the victim, parents, and students should report to the Office for Civil Rights within 180 days.

3. If you still feel the truth is not heard and proper justice has not been served, send a report to the US Department of Justice. However, this needs to be reported to the Department of Justice in dire situations when nothing else is working through the school or the Office for Civil Rights. Nevertheless, the Office for Civil Rights and the US Department of Justice follow the same guidelines for discriminatory acts as outlined by the US Department of Justice, so most cases should end at the Office for Civil Rights report.

As we found out earlier, there is no law specific to bullying in the US education system. This is a major issue and can cause a lot of problems for future generations to come. More than

---

16 "US Department of Education," How to File a Discrimination Complaint with the Office for Civil Rights, July 21, 2016, accessed November 29, 2016, http://www2.ed.gov/about/offices/list/ocr/docs/howto.html.

ever before, there is an awareness of the bullying epidemic in the United States. Furthermore, with the risen awareness on the issue and more organizations getting involved in educating students on what bullying is, its effects, and promoting antibullying, the need for bullying laws in the United States has a high chance of being implemented in schools and the government. Bullying does not only occur in school settings, but it may also be where most bullying occurs. Bullying can happen to anyone at any time, and therefore, laws specific to bullying are a need in the United States. Anyone who follows news on the bullying movement knows what is going on to bring awareness to bullying and what people are doing to prevent it. Bullying laws need to be created and implemented for schools and outside school settings. School officials should enforce the laws as needed, not just follow policies that they may or may not have in the school setting. Law enforcement plays the same role for kids that are getting bullied outside a school setting, and proper laws should be enforced depending on the type of bullying and the extreme of the bullying.

Bullying is an issue that may never end; however, everyone should be educated on what bullying is. As I have pointed out, some bullying may be discrimination as well as racial and religious stereotyping. Racial and stereotyped bullying is definitely on the rise for minorities, especially Muslim students. No student should be scared to practice their religion in school and public settings or feel they need to be one way at home and in school. Everyone should feel safe to get an education. Students facing bullying are most likely doing worse academically than students who do not get bullied, and it should not be as such. Minority groups, especially Muslim students, are now at the forefront of getting bullied and being scared to practice their religion in school. In many ways, they are being forced to live a double life, and these forms of issues need to be addressed.

Some of the major movements toward bullying awareness and prevention have been made through organizations such as Stand for the Silent,[17] Be a STAR Alliance,[18] and the 2011 Bully Documentary by Lee Hirsch, simply known as the Bully Project.[19] With something like Be a STAR Alliance and what World Wrestling Entertainment (WWE) does with Be a STAR rally in schools is an amazing way to bring awareness to bullying. These forms of movements and education on our kids need to be implemented along with the other things I brought awareness on and suggested. Through this effort, we are promoting antibullying, minimizing bullying, and educating students. With kids being educated on these issues, they know better before acting on their emotions and anger. Furthermore, to better our schools in the fight for minimizing or ending bullying, we can have peer counselors that students can go to for help. We might be able to get help from Be a STAR Alliance and have a student representative of the organization in the school that can shadow or work with counselors and deans who stand for the values and principles the organization promotes and follows. Through this effort, students can come to these representatives for help and guidance and report incidents if they do not feel comfortable with administrators and school officials. From there, the student representative of the organization would aid

---

17 End Bullying with Stand for the Silent," Stand for the Silent, 2010, accessed November 26, 2016, http://www.standforthesilent.org/.
18 "Be a STAR," WWE Community, accessed November 26, 2016, https://community.wwe.com/diversity/programs/be-star.
19 "The BULLY Project," The BULLY Project, accessed November 26, 2016, http://www.thebullyproject.com/.

and follow-up with whomever they report to and make sure the case is taken care of properly and with proper justice for the alleged victim of bullying.

In the twenty-first century, bullying has become one of the biggest, if not the biggest, epidemics affecting most students in the United States. Throughout a child's life and their schooling, most students face some form of bullying. Furthermore, at different times, they may be the perpetrator, victim, or bystander. Nevertheless, the goal is to prevent bullying, and everyone has a role to play. Since 9/11, minorities have been experiencing racial and stereotyped bullying. We now more than ever have a chance to create bullying laws in our schools and the government. It is not enough to have school policies to prevent bullying. We need strict laws that need to be properly implemented by school officials, and everyone, including school staff members and parents, need to be educated on bullying and learn what to do to help their children or the students who are facing bullying. It is not just the victims that need help but also the perpetrators to prevent bullying. Bystanders need to know what to do when they see someone getting bullied and made fun of. The bullying movement is currently going on, and in the future years to come, there is a lot more we need to do to prevent bullying. Bullying may not be an issue that can be completely stopped but bullying prevention must happen. The US Department of Education, Office for Civil Rights, and US Department of Justice are there to bring justice to bullying that may be a form of discriminatory bullying or racial and stereotyped bullying. However, as parents and students, it is our duty to be informed of the resources that we can count on and report to officials when we get bullied or discriminated against by our peers and educators.

Parental and family influence impacts the overall way a

child becomes. As parents, you are responsible for making your children understand the negative impacts of bullying and that it is never right to bully anyone. This is a principle that should be required to be taught from when they are a child. Do not wait until before middle school and high school start but from the start of schooling. It is a known fact that most children face bullying in our schools, so teach your child from the youth.

Families and a Student's Education

In a student's education, there are many factors that play a significant role in shaping the student's life and his/her education. A student's education is impacted by all his/her influences, and above all influences, the first and foremost influence is from the parents and his/her immediate family members. We can go debate about who has the biggest role in a student's education. However, the truth of the matter is that all parties play an equal role in his/her education. Among all influences, a child is first taught by his/her parents and immediate family members. Therefore, the teachings, valued morals, and principles instilled in a child, their upbringing and life principles from parents and family members, are all crucial in shaping him/her.

The parents and family's role in raising a child and more specifically his/her education is to teach the right moral values of life and principles in the home, so it is reflected in school and social settings. However, more than that is to be actively involved in the child's life and school activities. As parents and family members, to take the responsibility of your child's education means that you should be willing to be there for your child. The growth and development of a child also should include the community in your neighborhood and local district. If the goal of a child's education is for him/her to be successful in school, it is up to us to do everything we can to make sure our children are actively involved in their schools and community. As a community, we must make sure we have facilities for children to learn and parents to educate.

What we may see sometimes is that all children, especially in the youth, should simply go to school and come home, possibly an after-school program that may be available to them. However, what are we doing as parents and family members to get the most out of our community for our children? For the healthy development of children, we have to make sure we are able to provide our kids enough facilities for them to constantly be involved during their free time. Many kids may just come home and do their homework and then spend the rest of the day just watching TV. However, this makes our children's lives stale and boring. They would not know what to do since we never got them involved in extracurricular activities from their early years in school. These forms of activities that should be used as a resource may not be an everyday thing, especially not on a school night after coming home, but it is crucial to, at least, get the kids involved in these community-based activities on the weekends. Not only will they be outside of the house and not be bored, but these forms of activities help children develop in a healthy way. Furthermore, for them to be encouraged and motivated to excel in their studies, to see their parents and families involved would help with school achievement and school success.[20]

For us to further understand the importance of parents

---

20 National Education Association, *Parent, Family, Community Involvement in Education,*

and family's role and involvement in a child's education, we have to look at Joyce Epstein's framework on involvement.[21] Epstein's framework on involvement outlines six types of involvement that are all crucial and apply to a child's education as well. Epstein's six forms of involvement are parenting, communicating, volunteering, learning at home, decision-making, and collaborating with community. I have already touched on the importance of parenting and collaborating with the community. As far as the other four ways, they are also done within the family and the community. As parents and family members, we should look to see how we can be involved in our children's education in school and what we can do to make a positive impact in the school to improve our child's education. An example of such is to be part of the school's PTA.

Being involved in our children's lives shows them we want the best for our children, and it makes them happy to see the support they receive from their parents and family members. Therefore, whether it be volunteering in the PTA, a local community bake sale, or a school soccer team, we have to be there through thick and thin for the children. Furthermore, we need to know how to communicate with the school community and our children to know what is going on in our school and student's progress. We have to also be able to communicate with the children. We cannot simply let our children just come and go from school to home. Many of us just let things be without ever hearing our children's feelings, problems, likes, and dislikes. We should be open to hear what our children want and make sure we abide by their wishes. If we are only accepting our own ideas, many of which that are outdated, we do not progress to

---

in PB11 ParentInvolvement08 (Washington, DC: National Education Association, 2008), http://www.nea.org/assets/docs/PB11_ParentInvolvement08.pdf.
21 Ibid.

how things are in the twenty-first century today.

Furthermore, as far as learning at home and decision-making are concerned, we should be setting realistic goals for our children in their academic and personal lives. Families may have unrealistic ideas of success in education, many of which are those that parents and families are used to from their native country. We should be flexible with what we expect from our children and not pressure them and stress them with unrealistic goals. A lot of families, especially depending on the culture they came from and the expectations these parents grew up with in their motherland, have unrealistic, perfect mind-set type of goals for their children with grades in their assignments and tests. We'll come back to this later. These are goals and discussions that need to be discussed at home—outside of assisting the children's homework. There is much more than just a child's homework on a day-to-day basis that parents need to be involved in. Lastly, for decision making, we have to understand and work together to make decisions about our children's education in our homes, schools, and the policies and governance of the school system. Many parents and family members do not know what is going behind the scenes of our schools. The stakeholders of the education system are people sitting in an office in our state government offices. However, many parents are simply accepting of whatever comes to them while, all this time, they do not even know they could be actively involved and be advocates by going to education hearings and providing a voice for our schools and kids. Parents and families need to be informed of these hearings so they can make plans for these opportunities when they are available.

As a parent and caregiver, if you are not involved in your child or family member's education, how will anything change for the better? Parents and family members tend to make up excuses and stop themselves from getting involved in their children's own education. Therefore, we then hear excuses regarding demanding schedules, attending school activities, and having uncomfortable feeling.[22] Other issues we hear are the frustration with school bureaucracies and its policies, as well as language difference and the lack of understanding because of it. At the end of the day, whatever we say to ourselves about the hindering of being involved in our children's lives, we will only have ourselves to blame when something happens that does not benefit us and the students. As a school system, they are held responsible to relay the information of what to be involved in, what is going on in the school and the community, and what may be available to the children in all languages. As parents and caregivers, you have to be go-getters and must show an effort to school administration that you are there to not only be involved in the student's education but the school itself and the overall education system. The issue with language differences is the school and educational jargon, but many things are much easier these days since most things are available in the common languages of our society.

Outside of the parent's and family's involvement factor of student's education, there are certain issues that families are stuck in or have to struggle through to get through for a better life in the future and an education to be somebody. This is considered to many as the American Dream. For those that face these issues of poverty and the need to go to school, there is a need for education intervention and school readiness that

---

[22] National Education Association, *Parent, Family, Community Involvement in Education*, in PB11 ParentInvolvement08 (Washington, DC: National Education Association, 2008), http://www.nea.org/assets/docs/PB11_ParentInvolvement08.pdf.

are crucial to their upbringing and their education.[23] Poverty not only has an impact on a child's education but with long-term socioeconomic disadvantages, it affects factors such as psychiatric disorders, social and academic functioning, and one's physical health.[24] Poverty is a child's biggest demon on factors such as health, home life, schooling, and neighborhood. Furthermore, it is well-documented that the six major factors related to poverty that impact a child's development in general are the following: (1) poverty, (2) the depth of poverty, (3) duration of poverty, (4) timing of poverty in terms of age, (5) community settings (e.g., neighborhood and school setting), and (6) social network.[25] These factors make up a child's daily life, and it is important for children to be in the best condition possible. Nevertheless, as parents and caregivers, use the resources available to you if you face the issue of poverty or anything close. Do your part of maintaining the best lifestyle for your children at home, and the community and school should be the resources to help children facing poverty. No issue, regardless of how big or small it is, should stop a child from receiving an education.

In the fight to closing the achievement gap for students in the US education system, there are three factors that play a role to make sure children have the best outcome possible in all areas of their education: the parents and family, the community, and the government. As a nation, we have limited control of what goes on in our community and how to better it for our children unless we work together to make sure the resources are available. As parents, you have complete control on how

---

23 HB Ferguson, S Bovaird, and MP Mueller, "The Impact of Poverty on Educational Outcomes for Children," *"Paediatr Child Health"* 12, no. 8 (October 1, 2007), accessed December 3, 2016, https://www.ncbi.nlm.nih.gov/pmc/articles/PMC2528798/.
24 Ibid.
25 Ibid.

you will raise your children and what actions you will take in raising your children and helping them to the best of your ability. Our biggest fight to close the gap is the government and what educational policies and changes they choose to make. However, we do have a voice and the right to vote and make an impact and change even in our government. With enough voices, the government is bound to hear us. However, we have to be actively involved in our schools and government. After parental influences come the teachers teaching our kids. As a parent, if you have an educated background and understanding of our education system and how it works, you can play a major role in guiding your children to the right path and overcoming educational politics.

There are multiple research findings that show us the impact a parent has on a child. A parent's influence does not only affect a child's school outcome but the overall school performance, a higher chance of attaining higher education, and proper behavior in school. However, the opposite effects and more issues come up from those that come from broken homes and difficult backgrounds.[26]

Aside from the family structure, socioeconomic status, and parental and family involvement, there are more personal issues between parents and children that they may be facing. Here are things that, as students, we do not appreciate facing and seeing our parents do. Some parents tend to compare their children to other family members. Parents, you should not be comparing your child to other members of your family or any of your children's peers. This only shows that you are not happy

---

26 "Family Structure and Children's Education," FamilyFacts.org, 2016, accessed December 3, 2016, http://www.familyfacts.org/briefs/35/family-structure-and-childrens-education.

with how your child performs, and you are only accepting one type of school performance. You should understand by now that your children do not have the physical control of their performance and grades in school. No students like being compared with others and would rather prefer seeing parents that are supportive of their children's grades, effort in school and their studies, and improvement. By reading the first chapter, you should know by now that education is a political game of statistical information for funding, and that grades and testing do not prove your children's full potential. As a parent or family member, just be supportive and happy with your children's effort, improving grades, and their future academic endeavors.

Furthermore, a major issue facing some students from their parents is parents that expect perfection, and then the students become that perfectionists they are influenced to become. In psychology, one of the biggest lessons you learn and are told as a student is to not be a perfectionist. As a perfectionist or a parent only accepting of a short range of a high score, you are putting too much stress on children and their grades. The job of children is not to be perfectionists, but to do their best in their academics. For instance, let's say, as a parent, you are only accepting of your children to receive grades between 95–100. Think about the unrealistic expectation you have of your children. If the US education system followed the portfolio-based education system, then it would be more reasonable to expect that from your child, being if the education system followed what I outlined in the first chapter. Being a perfectionist does not help your child in a way, rather it puts a lot of pressure and stress on the child. Next thing you know; they are stressing out over even with the small things. Whether you are reading, this as a parent or as a student, have realistic expectations and goals that you consider for your academics. Have a proper range of grades (i.e., 85– 100) that you are accepting and are satisfied with. However, if you or your child does not receive that grade, don't be discouraged, it should only motivate you to do better next time and work harder for the future grades to come. Remember, you, as a parent or a student, are not in control of your grade in school—the teachers and the government are.

As a parent, the development of your children and their life, intellect, and educational success are highly dependent on the type of parenting you provide them while growing up. Some psychological facts of parenting that are well-known to be the best outcomes for parents and children are those with a strong attachment. The relationship and bond between the parents and children should be strong. Children should be free to talk about anything with you as a child. Sometimes, all they need is a friend, and they try to find that friend in you as a parent. Furthermore, there are four different parenting styles that are most common in the field of psychology: authoritative, authoritarian, permissive, and neglectful.[27] These parenting styles impact a child in different ways—some in positive ways and some in negative ways. Authoritative parenting is known to be the most recommended and effective parenting style. There is a balanced communication and a give-and-take in the decisions made between a parent and a child. It is not all about what a child says or vice versa with the parent. It is an agreement between the child and parent in which there is respect and compromised things set in place between the parents and the child.

However, unlike authoritative parenting, authoritarian

---

[27] "Types of Parenting Styles and How to Identify Yours," Developmental Psychology at Vanderbilt, December 10, 2013, accessed December 3, 2016, https://my.vanderbilt.edu/developmentalpsychologyblog/2013/12/types-of-parenting-styles-and-how-to-identify-yours/.

parenting is the complete opposite of authoritative parenting. Authoritarian parenting is demanding and strict. There is no flexibility or compromise like there is in authoritative parenting. In this form of parenting, there is very little room for a child to say anything and is set with strict rules and expectations.[28] Permissive parenting is another harmful form of parenting. Permissive parenting is those that are responsive to their children but do not have high expectations of their child's success. They are completely okay with how things are and let things be as they are. There is no motivation or effort from the parents for the children to do better in their academics per se. Lastly, as it says in its name, neglectful parenting are those parents that have no care for their children's needs. These parents may be completely uninvolved or abusive. The well-being of the children can be in question for such parenting. These parenting styles are highly crucial to understand because from the birth of a child, it is one of these parenting styles, depending on how you as a parent choose to raise your child impacts how your child will turn out.

    As a parent, you should always try to be an authoritative parent for your child's best outcome. Nevertheless, it is not the reality of this world and of parents. All parents have their own ways of raising their children and reasons on their way of parenting. We can only hope you try to be an authoritative parent if you are not. As a community, we have a responsibility of educating the parents on how to raise their children and use the family-based resources in our communities to make these forms of information and resources available to them. Parents that come from foreign countries may still only know or only be accepting of what is accepted in their motherland. However,

---

28 Ibid.

that form of parenting or child treatment may not be accepted in America. Aside from that, it may negatively affect the children's physiological self—along with their education in school.

The impact of parents and family in children's education may be more important and crucial than the children's actual schooling. Schooling for children starts in their home with how they are brought up, to the type of family they are brought up in. As parents and family members, we have to be there for the children and be actively involved in their upbringing, schooling, the community. No matter what hardships are faced, parents and family members are held responsible for the way their children turn out to be. Before we look at the school or the government, families have to make sure they are doing their part in being actively involved in their children's lives. A school education and the parent's and community's involvement consist of Epstein's six frameworks of involvements as mentioned earlier in the chapter. The challenges that come with parenting and family's involvement may be a socioeconomic issue, but the resources are available. It is crucial for families to be aware of the resources available or be the go-getter to obtain the governmental resources. Lastly, the way we choose to raise the children before and during their school greatly impact their personal and school life. As parents, it is our responsibility to know the parenting styles and be accepting of the suggestions given from a professional or trained individual on raising a child. At the end of the day, nothing should stop a child from obtaining an education.

Learning with Disabilities

There are many different types of people and different groups and types of people that come to America to get an education, and we should make sure all forms of services needed are provided and customized for the best outcome of their education. Among all groups of people, students with disabilities may have much more to deal with than anyone. For those with disabilities, it is hard to tell how or when they might be going through a difficult time, especially if we do not know they are diagnosed with something. In other words, some are diagnosed with a disability, and there are services for them in their school/college. However, there may also be individuals who have not been properly diagnosed or are not properly diagnosed and may face unimaginable learning disabilities. Regardless of the case or the disability, a community has a right to an education, and there are always new forms of disabilities that are being discovered, or an existing disability may be changed by the American Psychiatric Association (APA) in their publishing of the *Diagnostic Statistical Manual* (DSM). We have come to a point in the disability community where we should rethink how we define learning disabilities that students face during their schooling, and we should make sure we have understood the individuals and their disabilities and provide services as needed.

Student's learning disabilities are categorized as specific learning disabilities and related disorders.[29] This is understood as specific disabilities students have for learning and the related disorders of them. The specific learning disabilities are disabilities such as auditory processing disorder, dyscalculia, dysgraphia, dyslexia, language processing disorder, nonverbal learning disability, and visual perceptual/visual motor deficit. The related disorders are things such as ADHD, dyspraxia, executive functioning, and memory.[30] The learning disabilities for students are impacted by the mind. It may be that a student got their disability or disorder naturally or through a traumatic event. To understand how our brain functions, you need to know the function of the right and left hemisphere. It may be that one of the hemispheres is deficient to the other side. The right hemisphere is known as the creative mind. The functions of the right hemisphere are things such as creativity, artistic work, the imagination, intuition, holistic thoughts, music awareness, etc... On the other hand, the left hemisphere is known to be the technical side of the brain. Its functions consist of analytic thought, logic, language, reasoning, science, math, numbers, and skills, etc...[31]

A student's ability to perform well in school is the ultimate expectation of any educator. However, what if the student is not able to perform well on a subject? Let us say the student studies, gets tutoring, and does the work given to him/her; however,

---

29 "Types of Learning Disabilities," Learning Disabilities Association of America, 2016, accessed December 9, 2016, https://ldaamerica.org/types-of-learning-disabilities/.
30 "Left and Right Brain Function," MyShrink.com, 2006, accessed December 11, 2016, http://www.myshrink.com/left-right-brain-function.php.
31 Ibid.

a subject cannot process through internally for the student to perform well on it. What then? This is a harsh reality for some students. No matter how much he tries to internalize the info, a student does not understand the work given to him/her. This can be thought of as a disorder in the brain. The brain is deficient in understanding the subject for the student to do any satisfactory work. This also can go back to playing a role of the hemispheres in the brain, and two subjects to compare would be mathematics for the left hemisphere and English for the right hemisphere.

Furthermore, to continue with the example, let us say the student is right hemisphere dominant, and his left hemisphere, when it comes to certain subjects like math, is weak. Therefore, he is not able to do any satisfactory work in math. How do we help these kinds of students? In our disability community, we are currently diagnosed through the *DSM-5*, and what the *DSM* would say is the student may have a specific learning disorder with impairments in mathematics. However, the reality may be much more than that. With changes in the *DSM* and the latest publishing in 2013, what was once known as mathematics disorder is now gone. What was described for a student with extreme difficulty in math should be considered mathematics disorder, but it is no longer just an impairment for the student. Mathematics disorder now has multiple factors[32] for it to be considered a disorder. However, the reality of the education students gets these days is that they may not comprehend a subject. Therefore, what we should do with such students comes into question. They have ultimately gone through this inability to perform in a subject. After proper evaluation, they become part of the disability community. In these forms of

---

32 "Mathematics Disorder," MedlinePlus, December 2, 2016, accessed December 12, 2016, https://medlineplus.gov/ency/article/001534.htm.

situations, what we have are new disabilities of these students. Furthermore, what we have to accept about the reality of these situations is that the disability may randomly pop up for the students unexpectedly. I believe students should be able to opt-out automatically of taking the subject completely. In its replacement, they should either be awarded credits in the subject that their disability hinders them from taking or have it replaced with something else for them. We have in the disability community for those diagnosed with mathematics disorder to be opted out of the subject; however, it may be a little difficult to consider for an opt-out for a student with how things are defined in the *DSM-5*.

Moreover, in psychoeducational evaluations, we should reevaluate how we determine certain diagnoses and, more specifically, the type of testing given to a student during the evaluation. What we see is basic to hard material that is not a student's grade-level work. These evaluations are used to see if they are to perform basic stuff in reading, writing, and math. However, what needs to be given is the level of work that matches their grade level. Yes, we must test for basic understanding and ability to do work. However, the student's grade-level work should also be evaluated. If a proper evaluation of grade-level work is not conducted, we may not tell the true difficulty a student is facing with the work.

Furthermore, we should check to see the answers the child gives in these tests. After each test, if we see a child gets most or all the work to be wrong, this should be a red flag of a disability. We should see if the child does the work but can do it correctly, especially after explanations and examples. The examples may be in an academic setting rather than an evaluation center. However, regardless of where the work is done, it is a red flag for a disability if they make constant mistakes. This form of disability may be rarely seen with what I am describing, but it is a reality of many.

Another change in the disability community we should see in academics is students who are learning a foreign language. Similar to math and science, language learning is through our left hemisphere. It is a known fact that language learning comprehension is best done during the youth.[33] Cognitive and neuropsychology courses are about how the brain works and brain pruning, which is a major factor in language learning. In simple terms, our neurons and axons play a major role in language learning due to how they work. As a child, the brain is wide open, ready to take in information. Therefore, it is so easy for an infant to learn a language from birth. They start picking up on their native language from when they are in the womb, and it is a lasting effect at the age of three.[34] However, as you grow older, your brain starts pruning, and your neurons and axons cannot store as much complex information as a second language. A person who is not of the native tongue and goes to study a second language would have difficulty picking up and comprehending the language in their teenage and adult years.

Furthermore, when it comes to learning an entire language, a person has to pick up and understand the information being taught. He/She does not even understand what is being taught in class and how something came to be. Every person is different, and the ability to understand, comprehend, and be successful at

---

33 "Learning a Second Language Is Good Childhood Mind Medicine, Studies Find," Cornell Chronicle, December 12, 2016, accessed December 12, 2016, https://www.news.cornell.edu/stories/2009/05/learning-second-language-good-childhood-mind-medicine.

34 "Language and Literacy," The Urban Child Institute, 2016, accessed December 12, 2016, http://www.urbanchildinstitute.org/why-0-3/language-and-literacy.

language learning plays with two major factors: understanding and comprehension of the language when taught and remembering the taught material and satisfactorily performing well in school tests. By the time we are adults, it is most difficult to pick up on the language unless we already know it or have been learning it from high school. Nevertheless, the situation of being able to learn a language can change at any moment. From my experience, I can tell it may even come to the point of not understanding the language and how conjugations were made.

Language learning does not mean just remembering words of the language. However, for us to be successful in language learning, we have to be able to understand the basics of the language, understand the conjugations and changes of the type of words and know how to use that information to create a full, proper sentence based on the rules of the language. We cannot just look up each word of a sentence and write the word in that language. This experience may be extremely confusing and highly difficult for students that are not wired to that language by the time they are in their adulthood. I define this as a new disability for the disability community and, more importantly, the American Psychological Association (APA) to consider. I call this form of disability language learning dyslexia.

Language learning dyslexia: *the inability to understand and learn a foreign language at any age, especially during adulthood. A student's understanding and comprehension of the foreign language is limited for them to perform at a satisfactory level and has extra difficulty in the foreign language. The disability may vary person-to-person in a spectrum based on how well they can learn a language.*

Language learning dyslexia should not be confused with a

student with regular dyslexia and is trying to learn a language. Currently, that is where we are in our field of psychology. Even if we are to look at psychoeducational evaluations, there is no testing to test a student's ability to learn a language. Hence, why do we not have an official diagnosis of students who face a highly difficult time learning a language? That needs to change. The APA should create a test for language learning to see if one may have language learning dyslexia. Once again, like testing for math, as I suggested earlier, for foreign languages, it should not be determined by simple words or terms but a little advanced material of foreign languages during testing because that is the reality of classroom settings. We are not stuck with simple everyday terms but more advanced words and sentences as the semester moves along.

My concluding thoughts for language learning dyslexia is that we are in a state where there is no testing for language learning to see a student's ability to learn a language to determine if he/she may have a disability. If anyone hears of language learning dyslexia, they may understand the concept, but no educator can help. Nevertheless, if students feel that they cannot learn a language and can explain it through their experience in their foreign language class and class grades, they may be able to get a foreign language exemption from the office of AccessAbility. What was once an ability may no longer be an ability. Furthermore, it would not be fair or right for children to go through that form of a difficult time to do possibly average or less than average work if they cannot perform satisfactory work. There is a physical inability that is stopping the person from learning a language.

Furthermore, my suggestion to the disability community, any disability advocacy organization and the APA is to make foreign language a requirement for elementary school. That is right; I am saying to make foreign language a mandatory class from when children are in grade school because, as we have seen, they can pick up language from their youth more than their adulthood. Students should learn foreign languages, and it is an essential thing to live in this world. However, they need to be exposed to foreign languages from their youth at an early age. They have their native language taught at home, English from kindergarten, and all I am saying is to add on another foreign language from possibly the first grade, so they have the best shot at picking up on a foreign language rather than what most are now introduced to in middle and high school. Suppose language learning dyslexia is a reality for a student. In that case, an educator will pick up on it when it starts and hopefully starts the process of getting them evaluated for exemption if language learning dyslexia ever becomes an official diagnosis in the field of psychology.

  The resources available for students in school for those that have a disability are integrated co-teaching (ICT) classrooms, special education itinerant teachers, and accommodations as needed. There is the office of AccessAbility that looks out for the disability community in their colleges. These are vital services to students that any students with a disability should use and be required to regardless. As a student that may have a disability, never leave the reality of your situation a secret. Go to the office of AccessAbility to inform them of your condition and see what services they offer. They will provide you with the needed recommendations stated in your psychoeducational evaluation but may be able to help with other things outside of academics.

  The rights to an education for a student are given by the civil rights acquired throughout history. Multiple civil rights protect them, so they do not face any discrimination. Furthermore, just as the US Department of Justice protects students from discrimination, the disability community is also protected and given a right to education. Some of the major civil rights acts for disabled students are under the American with Disabilities Act of 1990 and Section 504 of the Rehabilitation Act of 1973. For the American with Disabilities Act of 1973, the rights of students with disabilities fall under Title II and Title III of the act.[35] There is also the Individuals with Disabilities in Education Act (IDEA), in which the Department of Education has the primary responsibility for enforcing IDEA. Also, once again, just like how the civil rights division of the US Department of Education protects discrimination in the school system for students, they protect the disability community through their rights.

The process to report any form of discrimination in the school system should be the same as mentioned in chapter three. Those three steps should be taken to the extent as needed. At many times, there may be discrimination either by peers of a student with a disability or an educator. Regardless of who it is, a report should be made. Any form of discrimination or bullying may be far worse for a student with a disability than one without a disability. The perpetrators will not know what they are dealing with and the effect of it on the students.

In the twenty-first century, the disability community is at a point where they are provided with services, whether it be at school, home, or in a professional environment; they are accommodated too. The education system and the disability

---

35 "2010 ADA Regulations," Information and Technical Assistance on the Americans with Disabilities Act, March 1, 2013, accessed December 9, 2016, https://www.ada.gov/2010_regs.htm.

community provide the services listed in a student's IEP or a psychoeducational evaluation report. However, as we have discovered, there is always a chance that new forms of disabilities and their proper accommodations can come up. The education system and the APA have to be prepared for it. The APA came out with new versions of their *DSM*, (*DSM-5)* being the latest installment of the manual. With new manuals, there also comes changes as to how certain disabilities and disorders are categorized.

For the future of the disability community and their education in the US education system, a student's perspective on his/her difficulties in subjects should be considered in high regard. It is always possible that a psychoeducational evaluation or the IEP does not tell us everything about the difficulty a student is facing. If a student expresses difficulty in a subject or a constant form of failing test grades is observed by parents and educators, they should be on high alert and immediately get the child tested to see the reality. I would love it if all parents and students agreed to get yearly psychoeducational evaluations before the school year starts to see if there is any disability of a student. However, that is highly unlikely because all parents would not agree to such a thing. Therefore, I suggest immediate testing if there is a negative trend seen in a child. A child should be evaluated before it's too late.

New forms of disabilities and new evaluations for subjects that are currently not available should be created. We can see that in my example of language learning dyslexia. Furthermore, without considering these forms of new disabilities, we would not grow as a community and would not help students with disabilities to their full extent. We rely so much on the evaluation that we do not take the student's verbal explanation of their struggles outside of what is said during the evaluation. While there may be bias on accommodating students simply by their explanation of struggles in their academics, if their grades correlate to what they express, I believe they should be given the proper accommodation.

The way to evaluate student's need to opt-out of a subject should be through multiple factors. If their psychoeducational evaluation says they need to opt-out of a subject, they are getting out of the course in place, possibly, an extracurricular activity or a different class to cover their credits or just opting out. However, if someone opts out of a subject, they may not receive credit for the subject. This can delay graduation, so once again, something should be given to replace the credit to show up in their school records and the report card or transcript. The opt-out process should also include student's expression of their difficulty in the subject correlating with their grades. If the brain cannot process the information on a subject, the value of students taking the class is pointless. If students cannot perform well in class, it will only hurt their class grades and overall GPA. For reasons like this (as I had said in the first chapter), although everyone in America may have the right to an education, they do not have an equal opportunity to be successful in the American education system.

The future of the disability community in terms of education is currently unsure. While there is no issue in terms of their right to an education and the accommodations they are required to receive and are receiving, there is always a chance for new forms of disabilities and disorders to pop up in the community. Moreover, the assurance of looking into new forms of disabilities is uncertain. At most, what we can expect currently is the APA looking at the disabilities and disorders we already know of and making changes or defining those differently for the future *DSM*s similar to the changes from the *DSM-IV-TR* to *DSM-5* was made.

Furthermore, students who may not have a disability or disorder to start with can randomly start having a disability. Disabilities are not something that anyone can ever be assured of if they will ever have one or not. However, a disability may come at any time to a student. As a community and those in psychology, we must continue the research for new education-related disabilities and disorders and be open to research the possibility of a new form of disability that is thought of given a proper understanding of what the psychology field is researching about and testing for.

The Administration

Everyone from the school principal, vice-principal, deans, counselors, office administrators to the security guards protecting our schools, colleges, universities, and private daycare directors all play a role in the school administration and in serving the student's education and the system. These are the people who maintain everything going on in our schools and keep a controlled situation in our learning institutions. They play a crucial role on a day-to-day basis to make sure every student can go through a school day and take care of all the challenges. However, with everything that goes on in the schools, the guidance for the students and management is making sure everything is done properly and in time to meet deadlines and demands for the school and, more importantly, to secure the education for the students.

Even though the school administration is to maintain the proper education of students, there may be many factors that impact the performance of the school and the students in the school. An educational administration needs to be effective, and it consists of many factors for the administration to run. However, many issues negatively impact the administration. These issues consist of leadership, communication, disconnection, partiality, and politics. In a school administration, some issues impact the students and issues that impact school administrators. These are issues that mainly impact students in some way.

For any administration or any corporation to work, the leadership of the administration must be strong. A leader can be unbiased, assess situations, and make a decision for a company or, in this case, the educational institution. In a school setting, we automatically look at the principal as the leader of our schools. If there is no strong leading principal, the school administration is bound to fall. Therefore, not everyone can obtain a position like the principal of the school. However, people tend to work their way up to that position during each school leadership transition. The educational administration, not just the principal, has to adhere to the policies set forth and make sure it is followed; and if any training or improvements are needed, the changes are properly made. They cannot allow their personal beliefs to impact a decision that impacts the students and the school.

As an issue in the US education system, communication applies to school teachers, administrators, and students. Effective communication in the school system administration is important, and there should be time to get all information to teachers and school administrators. A simple general meeting is not enough for effective communication among school administrators and teachers. Teachers and students need to have that face-to-face interaction to make sure all information is communicated, and everyone must know what to do so there is no issue how information is related to school administration and teachers and teachers and students.

Disconnection is interrelated to communication because it is the disconnection between students and the teachers and how they can interact with their teachers. The disconnection can also be among school administrating colleagues. School administrators have to be on the same or familiar page and have the same information. The disconnection in our school system between students and teachers also is impacted by the technology age. As we see in our generation, everyone is glued to our technological devices, especially students, throughout their time in school and outside.

Furthermore, technology has also become part of our classrooms, whether it be a smartboard or a computer screen in front of our student's faces on a big screen. Through this, the disconnection or possibly the lack of understanding of the technology is on our teachers—many of which are of the past generation who are now required to learn and adapt to technology to teach students. Nevertheless, outside of any form of disconnection or a lack of communication in our education system is the information related to students and its guidance. This issue between disconnection and communication will later be explained and analyzed in this chapter.

Partiality is an issue that is debatable depending on the situation of the student and the performance seen, and the struggles verbalized among a student, a parent, and a teacher, I would argue. Sometimes partiality is seen given to students who struggle in class but are giving their full effort to try their best and do their best in class. Therefore, sometimes a teacher may be lenient with the student and the grade he/she receives. Partiality should not be purposely given to just anyone.

If a student is truly struggling and the issues along with the effort are seen, the student should be given that little partiality to further his education and move on. Unfortunately, partiality can be formed with the current testing system through test grades that ultimately play a major role in the student's grade. However, partiality can sometimes be wrongfully abused for a student to receive a grade he does not deserve. Sometimes it is hard to tell if a student is truly having a hard time with a subject or a big hoax. We may even hear of favoritism, such as a teacher's pet, which can be a different form of partiality. Teachers need to be careful of those forms of partiality because someone who knows the subject and understands it may play a role in increasing his/her grade, even though his true grade is fine the way it is, and he does not have to worry about his/her grades. It is a simple issue of favoritism that builds up through nice acts between the teacher and student. However, in this case, if the teacher knows the student is doing fine, base his/her grade on what he/she is being graded on. Some students truly have an extremely difficult time than students that are naturally doing well in their class. You would not want students that are having a difficult time in class to suffer failure, even after all the struggles they are going through.

Lastly, politics impacts the position administrators are in. There are different antics certain administrators may use to have something fall in their favor.[36] We see these forms of issues in elected leaders and school boards. There is fierce competition between leaders for their policy to be implemented and gain that position. When things become a competition in these forms of cases, we lose focus on serving students and the school community. As far as elected officials are considered, they sit in a corporate office of the state capital building or their local office. However, most of these elected officials have no idea what is best for students for the success of their education. In college,

---

36 Ibid.

if you are a student leader of the college or the university, you may be able to have opportunities to go to your local community official in state and local hearing to voice your opinion. Parents, advocates, and students should all be able to go to these forms of hearing to speak up on issues they care about. Through these hearings, policies can be impacted, whether it be funding or other issues regarding the college or the education system. The students, parents, teachers, and other school administrators are impacted by these policies from the local board of education, state government, or federal government. Therefore, if these impacts you due to the politics of the US education system, you should voice your opinion and play a role in making a change.

Aside from problems in our educational administration that mainly impact our students and the communities, some issues impact the school administration itself. The American School & University[37] came up with ten major issues that schools may be facing along with recommended resolutions. While as students, we may not relate to the issues themselves, we understand and acknowledge that these issues exist in our education system. Every school has specific issues that it would like to address. The local official and the board of education are to address these issues.

Certain issues like funding are coming from the state since each state's schools are overlooked by the state government. There has to be a joint effort in addressing these issues, and the communities have to voice their opinion on the issues. These would also require them to be properly informed of the issues

---

37 "Top Ten: Issues Impacting School Administrators," American School & University, January 1, 2001, accessed December 16, 2016, http://asumag.com/mag/university_top_ten_issues

at hand.

Over the years, the expectations of students and teachers have increased in hopes of student achievement and teacher cooperation. Along with it, specific job duties and expectations are being put on principles, and the school administration is a central channel between the school district and the classroom. All of these and many forms of other engaged forms of communications between principals and school administrators to improve student achievement are due to the federal policies and initiatives and the Elementary and Secondary Education Act (formerly No Child Left Behind), and President Obama's Race to the Top grant.[38] These forms of initiatives are great to try to get students to do better, and it gives an equal responsibility on both students and teachers to make sure students do well. Ultimately, a teacher's goal is to make their students succeed in the classroom.

However, as times are changing, the need for administrators is becoming more and more important, and the adaptation of student's interest in the school system is becoming more relevant. Some of the consistent issues school administrations face consist of federal education standards, school budgets, overcrowded classrooms, and safety.[39] To start with the budget, it is an issue that goes through the local and state governments for each state. As mentioned earlier, advocacy through hearings is required in these situations, and the emphasis on the need for funding has to be explicitly voiced. The federal education standards and expectation is an issue that has been voiced and advocated for the change for years. It is not wrong to

---

38 "School Administrators: An Occupational Overview," Department for Professional Employees, 2001, accessed December 16, 2016, http://dpeaflcio.org/programs-publications/issue-fact-sheets/school-administrators-an-occupational-overview/.
39 Ibid.

want students to do much better than how students are doing. However, where is the motivation for it? To the end of high school, testing is a big percentage to determine a student's education standard. Standardized tests have become cancer to the education system, where it is a narrow measure of students 'achievement, and it may be difficult to quantify the full scope of principle influence on student's learning.

As far as overcrowded classrooms and safety are concerned, schools should look to have fewer students in each class. An average classroom holds about twenty-five to thirty students. Furthermore, there is only one way being taught for every single student. Therefore, while all students may receive the same information, we do not know if they completely understand everything. The way to benefit students in classroom settings is to have fewer students for teachers to have one-on-one time with them in the classroom. By having so many students in a classroom, teachers may not focus on each student personally or give more time to explain things to the students. Through this, we would be going back to the issue of disconnection, as discussed earlier. A student may feel disconnected from the classroom and the material being taught in the classroom.

Furthermore, for safety, administrators should make sure the safety policies are enforced to keep students safe from all forms of dangers, which is naturally done. However, some of the major issues regarding safety are students facing bullying and getting physically bullied. We also see these days that there is an increase in school shootings in our schools, and those issues are federally governed and dealt with.

School administrators and the students may come in

conflict depending on student to student. This issue brings us back to communication and disconnection, and it is the miscommunication and disconnection between a student and the administration of the school or college. Students in colleges experience this more than in a public school. While this issue between administrators and students in a college setting will be broken down and analyzed in the college experience chapter, we can touch it here. When students go to school administrators, they expect to be informed with the right information to make their lives easier and move along with their education. However, in what may be due to lack of staff training, some students may not be properly informed and get screwed by the school administration. School administrators must be well-informed of the student's information to be guided to the right place or given the correct information.

Staff training for school administrators should be regularly done, and testing of each department and office on some of the common issues students come with should be evaluated. Without keeping up-to-date with staff training, many staff members in these offices may be giving the wrong information to students, and it may drastically and negatively impact a student and his education. Staff members are supposed to know where to guide a student depending on what is asked of, not make it seem to the student they have to run around to get a simple answer. As administrators, you have all the student's general information, with everything from their name to test scores and so much more. A student should not suffer due to the administrators misinforming them.

The US education system's internal works in the schools are the school administrations that play a role in our schools. They are the ones to run the day-to-day administrative work.

The issues seen in the school administration system consist of leadership, communication, disconnection, partiality, and politics. These are issues that affect students and the communication and understanding between administrators, teachers, and students. Therefore, these issues can be seen between all parties depending on the issue and who deals with it. There should be clear communications among administrators. Students and parents are encouraged to be more involved in the political efforts to better our school system.

While some issues may be between students and the administrators, some issues directly impact administrators' daily proceeding in a school. As students, we may not completely understand it; however, we acknowledge that these issues do exist. However, student's issues due to the administration are what students can relate to and advise the US education system to improve in. School staff should be well-informed and be able to guide students in the time of their need. Administrators run the schools; however, misinformation or a wrong proceeding can greatly affect student's education.

The Price of Our Education

The United States, in many ways, has become the ideal place of education, with immigrants and Americans looking to get an education here as if it is the ultimate place for an education. Through it, people believe and receive the well-known concept of the American Dream. With education, there comes a financial price for individuals to receive an education. Even though we are in our schools as students, we may not realize the funding it takes to put a certain number of students in thousands in a school, let alone all the states or the United States as a whole. Education funding is through the school district or the dependent agency such as the state government. Currently, the expenditure of our school system is 63.2 billion dollars, which is 3.6 billion less than 2017 [40] when this book was originally published. The US education is continuously growing, and the funding is increasing with some exception to the U.S. budget and inflation for more students in this new millennial age.

Unless we look at the statistical facts of the US education

---

[40] 2021. *FACT SHEET: PRESIDENT TRUMP'S FY 2019 BUDGET.* [ebook] Washington D.C.: U.S. Department of Education. Available at: <https://www2.ed.gov/about/overview/budget/budget19/budget-factsheet.pdf> [Accessed 1 June 2021].

system, we do not see how the education system is becoming more and more expensive with the government needing to increase their spending for the US education system. However, we overlook this because it is a governmental institution in an office that is dealing with the spending of our education system. The finances of education do not impact students until we are looking to go to college or college. When we go to college, we get a reality check of how much our education costs. We spend a few thousand each semester in college to take a handful of college courses, which is when we take our education seriously more than ever. Once it impacts the students financially, there is a purpose to our education that we realize. Before college, our purpose and understanding of our education's importance and value come from motivational speeches from education advocates or our parents.

However, with our education, when we have to spend our education as adults, we can still get financial help from the government to help us fund our education. Some of the different forms of funding in college consist of FAFSA, Pell Grants like TAP, work-study programs, and scholarships. We may also be required to take out a loan when the financial help we get from the government does not cover it. However, these forms of federal funding (FAFSA, Pell Grants, TAP, and work-study programs) come with a price, and how much we receive depends on our family size and family income, among many other factors. When these forms of financial services are just not enough for us, it becomes difficult for students to go through college, and it may be a financial issue. However, through struggles, they find a way to manage them and fund their education.

As we saw earlier, funding for the education system is

constantly increasing, and without any doubt, with the current economic system we are in, the price of our education system will continue to increase over the years. This can become a burden on the students because it can limit a student on the number of classes they can take and manage it with the job they may have. It may also limit a student on when to go to class. Finances of education can limit a student to choose between taking classes a semester and working. Their education may be delayed because they may be paying the price of their previous class rather than just continuing with their education. Students who get financial aid and do not have to spend out of pocket for their semester or only have to spend a few hundred to cover the cost of their education can go through their education without ever stopping or compromising between taking classes for the semester just working. Every person is in a different situation with their finances and the price of their education.

The predictable future of the US education system with the current statistics tells us the price of the US education system that will only continue to grow. This may be due to multiple factors. We can easily tell its start with the economy and its effect on the finances of our educational institutions. We are just slowly rebuilding our economy. However, all we hear is the number of jobs being added each month, which shows a growth of our economy from the 2008 recession. However, we never heard from the government how it impacts the US education system. For those who do statistical research on the US education system and its finances who are seeing and reading reports on the educational finances, we would see that our system's price is continuously growing over the years. Just over the past fourteen years since 2002, we see a 36-percent increase in federal funding from $50 billion to $68 billion.[41]

---

41 "Federal Education Funding: Where Does the Money Go?" US News, January

That is almost a $20 billion increase; hence, we are now getting $70.7 billion in discretionary funding for the US Department of Education.[42] The more students receiving an education in the United States, the more the price of our education system will increase.

With the amount of money we are receiving in our education system, the price of the education system is not just financial but also in terms of the quality of the education. The quality of the education system should truly be thought of and emphasized by the government and those receiving an education. Parents, education advocates, and students have always expressed the quality of the education they are receiving, starting with one of the top issues previously discussed: standardized testing. However, if the government does not listen to our concerns and issues and does not change to better our education, it should give us an idea of where we are in our government and our education system. The price of the education system right now is a failure for many due to all the difficulties students face on a day-to-day basis. The quality of our education can be vigorously improved if those in power choose to make the changes required in our education system. Alternatively else, all we are doing is wasting our breath. The education system does not come up as a major issue in our government. It is not something we hear of regularly.

Throughout the years, we may hear of a new policy or initiative from our president to better our education system. However, these forms of quality-based improvement are not felt

---

14, 2016, accessed December 31, 2016, http://www.usnews.com/news/blogs/data-mine/2016/01/14/federal-education-funding-where-does-the-money-go.

42 US Department of Education, *Fact Sheet-US Department of Education*, in Funding Highlights (n.p.: US Department of Education, 2015), https://www2.ed.gov/about/overview/budget/budget16/budget-factsheet.pdf.

by every student in the US education system. Whomever the change or policy may fall on may see the change. However, there have to be federal- and state-level-based policy changes that impact the students of the United States and not just a particular group of people. While little changes and efforts come a long way for these students, there is no global impact for all students in the United States to be satisfied. While we can say, "You cannot make everyone happy," this is a matter of the quality and price of the US education system on the students going through it. Therefore, if we hear the voices of those advocating for change and make those changes, we can satisfy everyone in the US education system. There are certain changes and There are certain changes and issues like standardized testing and the need to stop it, impacting all of the United States and all its students.

Education funding, for the most part, falls on the state government in the US education system. The financial maintenance of our education system comes from the state government. Furthermore, along with it comes all the policies, rules, and regulations, what will be taught in each grade, and what will be covered. The government is at the top of this hierarchy, and the price of our education system all starts from the top in the state government and trickles down to the educators, administrators, and most importantly, the students in the US education system. Therefore, as we see, the price of our education is not only a financial matter but also a quality matter. It is us, the people, and our kids going through the US education system that gets the firsthand experience of the price of our education system. The quality of our education system is quite often compared to our counterparts overseas around the world. If we are to look at the rankings of the education systems worldwide, the United States falls to number fourteen in overall rankings, whereas South Korea is number one.[43] Our government should look into the education system of the other countries to see how they can improve our education system to better the quality of the education and make the changes they can.

During student's education, they may choose to start working and learn the world's reality and become more financially independent. For the most part, students can start working as early as age sixteen in the United States when they are in high school. From that point on, they start obtaining this understanding of the value of money and obtain work experience. They may do it to contribute and help their parents on a day-to-day basis; it may be that their financial circumstances may require them to, etc... The reality of the students turns out that they may need a job for them to survive in their financial situation.

Furthermore, sometimes students may choose not to have a job, such as cultural reasons or the importance of education put on them by the family. Therefore, the family may feel that having a job and going to school at such a young age may negatively impact their education. While that may be somewhat of an extreme, though, it may be a reality for many. In that case, we may have families required to live paycheck to paycheck and can barely make a living due to their financial circumstances. However, that is the sacrifice some families may put on themselves to make sure their child receives the best education possible. However, the reality may be that it would have benefitted the family or just the student himself/herself

---

[43] "The Learning Curve," Pearson, 2016, accessed December 31, 2016, http://thelearningcurve.pearson.com/index/index-ranking.

in the long run if he/she is to work. At the least, the interest and importance of having a job are understood and are not later negatively affected when the child goes into the work field and is looking for a job. He/she would not be shocked by the reality of the job market and the process of getting a job.

When it comes to college and the financial world, it is a shocker and a burden on many of the costs of a college education. The real price of college depends on several factors that families have to consider and remember before deciding with their child. When you are in high school, you may be thinking that financial aid will cover the cost of education. The reality is that there are multiple factors to consider that determine the yearly cost of an education for the average of twenty-four to thirty credits per year (twelve to fifteen credits per semester). For some students, the net price of their education system may be reduced through grants and scholarships. However, chances are the full price of the education has not been covered.

The sticker price of a college education depends on everything from what college you go to and where you live during your time in college. Some of the main factors to look at when determining what college to go to are tuition, fees, housing and meals, books and school supplies, and personal and transportation expenses. These are all the factors that determine the ultimate price of your education. Furthermore, this price can fluctuate year to year because, as we know, the price of education is always increasing. Currently, the actual price of a college education ranges from close to $10,000 to a little over $21,000 per year among all forms of institutions.[44] However, while that may be the average cost overall, the price of a college maybe,

---

[44] "Fast Facts," Tuition costs of colleges and universities, 2016, accessed December 31, 2016, https://nces.ed.gov/fastfacts/display.asp?id=76.

even more when you break it down to the types of institutions. For example, private nonprofits and for-profit institutions average about $24,000 to $36,000 in college tuition.[45] When we look at these statistics from the National Center for Educational Statistics, it should open our eyes to an understanding of how much is being spent toward our education and compare it to the quality of the education we are receiving. A debate that has been going on for a while about college education is the concept of a free college education.[46] As students, we may immediately go off and say, "Yes, we deserve a free college education." That thinking may be directly due to the financial effect on a college education. However, according to Andrew Kelly, there would be a public strain on budgets leading to shortages rather than increased access.[47] With a free college education, there would be an increase in students receiving a college education, and the public budget would then be impacted with a strain. We also have to think about the quality of education. While one may receive a quality-based education as much quality, we can get in the United States; others may not receive that same quality. Many resources would be in expenditure to serve the new students coming into getting an education.

Ultimately, this concept of a free college education brings us back to the reality of the US education system. We can realize the problems mentioned above that it is once again all about the funding an education institution receives by how students do in their institution. The funding of a college education would be in jeopardy with a free college education due to all the changes that would occur through a free college education. In one way,

---

45 Ibid.
46 Deborah Santiago, "Should College Be Free?" *The Opinion Pages*, January 20, 2016, http://www.nytimes.com/roomfordebate/2016/01/20/should-college-be-free/the-problem-is-that-free-college-isnt-free.
47 Ibid.

yes, a free college should be there to take out the strain of the financial burden off students. Students may even have more flexibility in choosing to have a job and not having a job based on their needs. There are so many students having a job and going to school at the same time. However, not all students are doing it to have a job. For many, it is their way of surviving and financing their college education. Furthermore, it is for them to finance their education and their everyday life as a college student. Through a free college education, students can choose to have a job and not have one for the best outcome of grades in school.

The education system, in ways, is almost like a job to students. We spend five days a week and about eight hours a day in school, just like how a real job is. For those in elementary, middle, and high school, that is the lifestyle they are getting. Furthermore, we are all required to come back home and spend a few hours doing our homework and studying on top of it. If you are in college, it is a similar situation—only the benefit is you get to make your schedule. Education is nothing more than a job when you think of it as such. The only thing is we are currently not getting paid to be in school. We may get back the grant money from our financial aid. Of all levels of school, whether you are in grade school, middle school, high school, college, or even higher studies, I would argue we should get paid by the government to be in college.

The idea of getting paid to be in college is wishful thinking that is not a realistic idea, but I am sure many students would love to get paid by the state or federal government to be in college. It can play as a positive reinforcement to be in college. I would argue that all students may not have the opportunity to work during their college tenure. By them working, it may negatively impact their studies. Not all students are the same, and in certain cases, we may hear of students that would love to work during their time in college but cannot because they do not have the time, or for them, their education comes first. Now, if we were to have every college student get paid a certain amount every year, students would not have to worry about financing their education by working. Students will once again choose to work if they wish to, even though they are getting paid every year to be in college. How much each student should receive is up for debate. However, at least a little over the average amount an individual makes working a minimum wage job. The government, in this case, would send a big check at the start of the school year for the student to their home, or they can receive the check-in from their school's financial aid office. Being paid to be in college would benefit everybody, make time to have a job, and choose not to have a job but would benefit from having one. However, how students use the money and benefit themselves to stay off the streets to be in class is a topic for discussion.

An average student in college spends a few bucks every day, starting with their morning coffee to their time going home. However, there are also exceptions for choosing to have the coffee at home and bring food from their home. Nevertheless, that is highly unheard of. These little expenses here and there build up, and we may find that students may not have made smart financial decisions. It may not be simply due to their daily spending, but it can be of many factors. What would benefit students is for them to have a proper financial education before and during college. Students should be taught the pros and cons of financial management. Students should be financially literate by the end of their high school when they actively spend money, whether it be money they get from their parents or through work. Good financial literacy would benefit students and make them financially conscious of their money and make them smart about saving their money, learning the pros and cons of finance, and reaching smart and wise financial decisions, especially during college.

A way for students to be financially literate is through Wise's Financial Literacy Certification Program.[48] Talking from experience for someone who has taken the program course in high school and has received my certification, I can say it truly teaches you every aspect of a person's financial life. You understand the ins and outs of finance management and learn the various aspects of financial literacy for you to be conscious of your finances. Similar—if not specifically that—programs should be available to all high school students in the United States as part of an economics class. While this certification may not be like you are set for life with finances, and you cannot mess up with your finances due to this certification, it is a confidence booster and a start to prepare you for the path of adulthood. Taking this program is perfect for twelfth graders since it is right before you go to college. At the least, with education through a program like this, you have a very useful resource in your back pocket. The US government should invest in having programs like this in high school for seniors to take.

For students, the biggest issue in their finances on how they choose to spend their money is their choices of needs versus wants. Students have to understand the concept of needs versus wants, especially when it is a financial matter. It does not matter what grade you are in—the expenditure of money

---

[48] "Wise (Working in Support of Education)," Wise, 2006, accessed December 31, 2016, http://www.wise-ny.org/programs.htm.

is done regularly by everyone. However, what you choose to spend your money on and when to spend it on is what you have to be conscious of. As a student, you are most likely broke and trying to make ends meet by having a job and contributing to your family's expenditure. However, it is up to you what you spend your money on and when you spend it. If you feel you need to spend money on coffee, lunch, and snacks every day aside from any other expenditure, you may do so, but then you are highly mistaken. What I am reinforcing is choosing what to spend your money on. When you decide to go spend money on something, you should ask yourself, "Is this something I need at this moment?" If it is not, then you most likely do not and should not spend money on it. Similarly, if you need to purchase something and you cannot live without it at that moment, and it is an emergency, then, of course, you should purchase it. It is small tips like these you can figure out on your own during your time as a student in your education.

The price of the US education system comes in many forms for a student and the government. The funding of a US education is through the state government in which the policies, rules, and regulations, what to teach, and when to teach it (what grade) are all determined by the US Department of Education and the state government. For the funding of a US education, the government spends billions in funding our education system. Along with it, there are government-funded financial resources for college students. The resources include FAFSA, TAP, Pell Grant, work-study, and scholarships, along with loans if they choose to take out a loan. The reality of students is that many students start working in high school at age sixteen. There can be multiple factors impacting their need to work. However, not all may be able to have a job, whether it be due to cultural reasons or the negative impact on their education.

While all students may not have a job during their education, hypothetically speaking, they should be paid for a college education. College can be extremely expensive, and everyone can benefit from getting paid for being in college. Some have a job during college, and those who may benefit from having one cannot do whatever their reason may be. If the government can pay every college student aside from the financial aid, they may receive. It would benefit all students financially and put them in a much better financial situation than we heard of. They would be clear of debt and clear of a loan by the time they finish their education.

The financial aspect of a student's education is a sticky situation where there are many aspects to think of, and to better the financial aspect, we have to look at the actual finance of the education in terms of funding, as well as the quality of the education students are receiving. The price of an education in the United States should be of equal value for a student's quality. At this moment, we need to better the quality of the US education system. For that to happen, it starts with changes that can be made by the state and federal governments and by hearing the voices of the students, parents, and education advocates. Countries overseas and their education should be evaluated to see how they are ranked so well compared to the United States and what can the United States do to change and implement better policies for an education that can meet the price of an education in the United States.

Preparing and Transitioning to College

The transition from high school to college can be a very confusing and difficult one or an easy transition depending on multiple factors. This is probably one of the biggest and one of the most important transition and time of your life. The hype of going to college itself is already made into a big deal as it already is. The preparation of getting into college may be really exciting and full of different activities that you do in and outside of school, alone and with your parents and family. However, the reality the students face and their first impression with college may be exciting but also unexpected or shocking. At the end of the day, everyone's experience is different, and the issues faced during this time that can be avoided for the students should be avoided. While you should be excited to go to college, the preparation and transition experience should be equally exciting and valuable.

When you are thinking about going to college, it starts with the preparation of going to college, which can consist of many activities academically and personally. To start off, let's talk about what goes on academically. The preparation of college starts in your junior year in the eleventh grade. First of all, there is this huge facade about how important your junior year is. In our schools, there is this emphasis on how the junior year is the most important year of your high school, similar to the emphasis you hear about the seventh grade when you are getting ready to go to high school. The eleventh grade consists of multiple standardized testing and extra time just on getting ready to go to college. It is The year you take your SAT or ACT is sometime in the eleventh grade.

The preparation of taking the SAT/ACT itself is very costly and time-consuming. It is just extra pressure and extra work, and by studying, you are required to put in time and extra effort as soon as you wish to start. Hopefully, you have started early in your high school tenure. These standardized tests become a major part of a student's life in high school because there is no other way to get to college. These tests play a major part in determining what college you go to. The tests are important, but does your school truly prepare you for such tests? You may be able to find a preparation class or information session, but most likely, you are spending out of your own pocket to prepare to take these tests. So the way the education system works is rather than your school truly preparing you for these forms of tests as part of the preparation of getting into college. They will give you the responsibility to find time outside of your school and academics and to go to a tutoring center to prepare yourself for these tests. Wouldn't it be better if your high school were to prepare you for the exams?

When it comes to these standardized tests that really test how well prepared you are for college, it should be the high school to prepare you for these tests. High school is a time where you take a few extra classes aside from your common core. You probably have an extra class like a shop class or some special program class like an ROTC program. Just as such, our education system needs to invest in what is really important. If we are really going to use the SAT/ACT as a major factor in determining the decision for our college, it should be equally valued in our school system and our high schools. The SAT/ACT preparation class should be given from the sophomore year in the tenth grade. That way, it gives students a good one-year-ahead preparation to prepare for the exam they will eventually take in their junior year. Having it from the ninth grade can be an option students have.

By having SAT/ACT preparation classes from the ninth grade, it may be a burden on students and extra stress. Students may not be interested since they just started high school. Having the option to have the extra class gives students an option, and it may be a way to help them in the future with their academics and classes. By having the SAT/ACT class in the ninth grade, it can also be used as an option for students to use as a replacement class for a class like a shop class that they are having an extremely hard time with or are just not interested in. Students need to have more freedom with the classes they have rather than just being told what to take when and making things mandatory for them. While this idea is more visible in college, it should start in their high school years with something like a SAT/ACT preparation class.

Aside from taking SAT and ACT exams for college, the other academic part of preparing for college is your actual academics in high school. Your high school GPA and just your grades in general are emphasized by teachers as grades that will follow your whole life. Ever had that being told by your teachers? That your high school grades will follow your whole life? As if high school grades even matter after college or when you apply for a job after getting out of college. The truth is the only grades that will matter most are your college grades. If you are trying to get a job right after high school or during high school, then it may count or have a little more emphasis. However, the truth is that your high school grades only matter to the colleges you apply for aside from your SAT/ACT grade.

Furthermore, in regard to academic work to prepare for college, there is a major issue with our education system in preparing students for the actual academic work and specifically writing on a college level that students fall behind on. When you are in high school, you are not taught to write on a college level in the eleventh or twelfth grade. Students then, when they go to college, are required to take their placement exams for reading, writing, and math. However, of all the subjects, writing is something students will do constantly in all their college courses. However, writing on a college level is not something students are prepared for. This is something I feel should have been taught in eleventh or twelfth grade English, if not the full year, at least half of the year of each grade. Writing is something college students will do the most of throughout the entire time they are in college and further studies and just in life in general. There is a huge difference between knowing how to write like a college student and how you write up to high school. My proposal is to prepare students to write on a college level from the eleventh or twelfth grade in their high school.

Furthermore, at the least, if students were prepared in high school for the difference between high school writing and college-level writing, they would get a head start in crafting their writing style and the foundation of being a great writer. They would not only be prepared to tackle their writing placement exam but would know how to write in college and in the future as they move along over the years. This way not only are they prepared for just their academics, but for life in whatever writing they do. The eleventh and twelfth grades should be used as a way to prepare students to be ready to take their placement exams. I will talk about the benefits of this and how this can help with the transition to college later in this chapter.

Outside of the academic portion of your preparation for college, there are things students should do on their own and with their family. Some of the classic things we hear about when someone is getting ready for college is the classic college road trip or moving out. Things like this should be encouraged more in other cultures than just the Western countries or cultures. Growing up, it seems as if only Americans get to do that. What I mean by this is that maybe only the American-born students get to have this independence of going through family or college road trips or moving out. However, that probably is the media misconception put on us from when we were kids. Nevertheless, there are definitely certain cultures that would not allow this to happen or find it to be perfect. For those parents and cultures that really don't give their kids or community that choice of freedom, I would like to speak to them.

As a parent, you have to realize you cannot baby your kids your entire life or wait until they are married to let them go. When they are considered an adult at age eighteen or twenty-one, let your children find themselves. When they are making the transition from high school to college, realize that they are all grown-ups, and it is time for them to make that transition from children and teens to adults. Similarly, when preparing your children for college, get them financially and mentally ready for college. As a family or as parents along with the college student have these college road trips or let your children move out of your house. There should be a line as to where to hold on to your culture or personal beliefs when it comes to things like this. Just because you were not brought up like how Westerners are brought up, given these forms of freedom choices, if they are available choices for your children, then let it be.

    First of all, in this matter, let your children live alone or in a dorm. If you keep thinking and worrying about every little thing during this transition from high school to college and stop your children from moving out or living in a dorm if the option is available, then you yourself are limiting the personal growth of your children. While what the media usually portrays is unrealistic in real life, there are certain things—like how the transition from high school to college should be—on a personal level for the child. It is something doable if you as a parent choose for it to be. You cannot just think the negatives and prevent your children or relatives from not living alone if they have the choice to. It can help the students in many ways, such as teaching them independence, responsibility, and being conscious of choices and decisions they make. That also does not exclude the fact that they will mess up time to time. However, they can always learn from their mistakes. Therefore, being able to live on their own in an apartment or a dorm or going out of state for college are things that should be highly encouraged by parents and family members if it's not already.

    Another exciting adventure the family can do together is the classic college road trip if you are expecting your child to study out of state. First of all, as family members and parents, be open and have that choice available for your child if you can afford it or if your child qualifies for it. It is not going to be a temporary study abroad program but actually a long-term thing for you and your child. College road trips should be planned for your child to see what college out of state or region you are used to or live in. Don't worry, parents, it's not the end of the world. Your child will return back home during breaks and maybe even weekends. However, let college road trips be a priority during this preparation and transition period.

As a student, other things you should do for yourself to prepare for college is know yourself, your likes and dislikes, your academic interests, and what you are good at. Remember that when you go to college, you are eventually going to declare a major that you are choosing as a career field for your future. There are too many cases of students going into college not knowing what they want to do with their life or what they are passionate about. What a lot of students do is go to college with a major in mind and later on change their mind and their major. Technically, there is nothing wrong in doing that. You have the freedom and choice to, but it also hinders you and puts you behind from your graduation. By the time you are in college, you should know what you are passionate about.

If you do not know what you are passionate about then use this preparation prepared while you are still in college to realize what you really want to do in life. However, this is a topic for another time, possibly one of the last chapters in this book. Nevertheless, I will tell you this: if you are truly passionate about what you study and want to do in your life, then you should stick with what you choose to do in college. You do not want to go to college trying to figure out what you want to do in life only by delaying your graduation or constantly changing majors. Changing a major would mean a lot of your previous major classes no longer count toward your 120 credits for graduation. Also, do not just change a major because it becomes challenging. Every major, at some point in all its classes, has its most difficult courses, and it won't always be your last few courses. There will be certain courses that hold a high priority in your major or what direction you choose to go with your major and your field of study. Therefore, the bottom line is for you to know yourself and your passion for what you want to study in college before getting into college and stick with it.

From the preparation of high school comes the transition of going into college. The transition to college can be somewhat surprising or shocking depending on what you end up with. When you transition to college, you are required to take placement exams in reading, writing, and math. This determines your level of proficiency in these three subjects. What happens to many students after taking these exams is they may end up in a remedial course because they are not well proficient in these subjects when they get out of high school. This is what I was referring to earlier about placement exams. These placement exams students take can often put back a student in taking a remedial course that has no value and is NOT credit-bearing courses. That means when you take a placement exam and if you do not pass it with at least the acceptable grade your college accepts, you are put in a remedial course that is not credit bearing only to retake the exam at the end of the semester. From there, you are taking an exam only to prove to the school you are satisfying enough to move on to a real course—the course you were really supposed to take if everything went as you planned.

The issue with remedial courses when entering college should have been something that was taken care of in your junior and senior year of high school. High school is the place that should have prepared you to be ready for the college level proficient in these subjects because these are what high schools should end up doing to help student's transition. Without the preparation, students are left unprepared to face college, and they end up having a bad experience in their first year. The personal experience itself may be very negative, but when it hurts them academically with something like a remedial course, that hurts even more. Ultimately, what I'm saying is our schools do not prepare you for college academically, even though they should be held responsible for it to. Especially for the subjects of reading and writing, it is definitely something students should have a good, solid foundation on and know how to pass the placement exams with a proficiency score but also really know for their own good, not just to pass a test.

With how high schools should prepare you to be proficient in college for you to do well in your reading and writing proficiency exams, the same cannot be said about math. The issue with math here is you may be degraded to a lower-level math in high school than just following the trend of regular high school kids that just keep on advancing to the next math level rather than being degraded to something lower if you cannot do well your first time around in what you were originally placed in. So in high school, you might go from taking math A, failing it, retaking it in summer school, and then after passing it in summer school, put in algebra class, then geometry, and end with trigonometry by your senior year in high school. It really all depends on how well you do in math. With math, there are levels, but with reading and writing, you may be left back a grade but never be put at a lower reading level than expected for your grade.

Other issues during the transition of college are the ways you are informed of information from your college administration after the welcoming to college. When it is time for you to apply for classes, it depends on what type of student you are, the general education requirement, and how well-informed you are. You start off with general education requirement classes in your freshman year. The first two years are really to make sure you complete all your general education requirement classes. If you are a transfer student and go into another class, there may be specific general education requirement courses you need to complete for the college. You have not even made your major official. However, if you have chosen a major before coming to college, you can easily be informed of the classes to take by talking to a counselor and your grades for your placement exams.

However, the issue with the transition from high school to college or college to college is the administration and how well they can inform their students. One of the issues students face, as it was touched on the administration chapter, is being misinformed by the administration. What students may have to do is be a go-getter and go to administrative offices to get the proper info. Sometimes what happens is that these administrative offices are not able to properly guide a student to the right office or give false info. A lot of students can get screwed by the administration like this. Students should not have to face the issue of being misinformed or misguided by the administrative offices of their colleges, as it can hinder the students and impact many things.

If students bring an issue to an administration office that should be able to answer their inquiry, the issue they face should be looked into carefully, not just be told to go to another office or a similar office that can also deal with the problem. Administrators need to be able to give clear-cut answers and not get students to just keep running around. We may not hear of these forms of issues, but issues like these are what students can face during the transition period of their colleges. These offices should be able to look at the placement exam scores of students, not just leave it up to the testing office for it to view them. From the placement exam test scores to what courses have been taken or need to be retaken are information many of these administrative offices, especially the registrar's office and admission office, should have access to and be able to inform students off. During the transition period, whether you are a freshman or a transfer student, these are most likely the major issues you may face from the administration.

    For students to make the transition to college easy, there are a few things the education system can do to help the incoming college freshmen and transfer students. As someone who comes to a new environment, it can definitely be an intimidating or scary experience. Therefore, one of the suggestions I have for the college's administration to implement in this transition period is to assign a one-on-one mentor to each new freshmen or transfer student. As a freshman, it is your first few days as a college student. While being in college does not mean for someone to baby you anymore, it would benefit a new freshman to get a mentor. The mentor should be chosen based on what the student plans on studying. A higher-class student that mentors the student should be of the same major as the student. If there is no major declared or the student does not know what he/she will study, then it can be anyone of their choice. The mentor should be assigned to the freshman for a year after the orientation so they do not fall into any trap and can easily get help with any issues he/she is having. The mentor can be a guide during the first year of college for the student. Therefore, the mentor should be helping the student everything from getting him/her accommodated to the college, the administrative offices, and most importantly choosing the right classes.

As a freshman, no student wants to fall into a trap or take classes he/she cannot manage in his/her first semester in college. Therefore, the mentor can be a guide to say which classes to take from all the classes available or recommended by a counselor. A rule we follow as college students from day 1 to balance out our classes is to take two hard and two easy classes. There are things such as choosing classes, choosing class sections with good professors, and learning about Rate My Professor and how that works. At the end of the day, a student can benefit from choosing these classes, but also coming up with a well-balanced class schedule in terms of timing and when the classes are available to take. Every freshman should definitely have a mentor for the first year of their college and get help with choosing classes, getting issues fixed from administrative offices, and lastly learning how to study in college to have a good GPA by the end of the first year. It would benefit in getting help through a mentor to start off their college tenure on the right foot with a good GPA.

Furthermore, just as how a freshman should get a mentor in his/her first year of college, a college transfer student should also get a mentor in his/her first year as a transfer student. While transfer students do have experience of college work, they still should get a mentor since they have transferred to a new college. Once again, just like freshmen, transfer students can benefit in getting guidance from a mentor of the administrative offices in the college, to get the proper guidance to get the correct info of where they truly are in their current college tenure, and what they need to take for their first semester at their new college. A lot of the times, what we see is students do not get the proper info for their major and classes to take and is given the runaround by the administration of the college. A mentor can help transfer students make the proper transition to their new college.

The preparation and transition time from high school to college can be an overwhelming experience, while it is also an exciting time for the new chapter to start in a student's life. From doing standardized tests to knowing what college you want to go to and what you want to study are things required for the preparation to get into college. There should be personal and family-oriented activities during the preparation to college. It is also a time to become more independent than you ever were. Every situation of the family is different, but a more independent life is a must no matter how much parents want to hold on to their child. The transition from high school to college can be a difficult one when you are getting into a new environment. There are many administrative issues that a student either as a freshman or a transfer student can go through.

The actual transition of getting into college whether it be a freshman or a transfer student to a new college should consist of proper guidance and mentorship. The administration cannot always be counted on. A mentoring program for freshmen and transfer students would benefit students tremendously personally and academically. There are a few tips that can be recommended to freshman and transfer students. As a new student in a college, immediately become well acquainted with the administrative offices and any special programs you may be part of. Do not be someone who just goes to college and gets out. Treat your college and the closest individuals you know either through your program or through the offices you visit most, as family. You will be spending about four to six years in your entire college tenure, get to know certain individuals in a personal and professional matter. Some of your best moments as a student will be if you become part of the college family. Administrative offices and professors are not just there to be some administrative figures. If there are people you get to know really well, you will feel like you are part of your college's student life. A lot more of this will be discussed in detail in the next chapter.

As far as academics are considered and college politics and issues are concerned, you basically have to be a go-getter. You may be running around at times, but you have to do that sometimes, especially at the beginning of your time in a new college. In the beginning, it can be confusing during the transition; however, you must be able to take charge and do whatever it takes for you to be ready for your first semester in college. No one will be there to baby you or do anything for you. The administration will only give you the info you need. But the actual work and time needed to be successful in college is on you. The preparation and transition of college can be a confusing and frustrating one at times, but you have to make the best of it by putting in the time and work needed for you to be ready for your first semester at a new college.

The College Experience

The US college experience can be very enriching and enticing as things are illustrated by the media and all the movies and shows we watch daily. Going from high school to college, you might think about all the things a college has and what it consists of. While much of what we see in the media, movies, and shows are there, the reality of what it takes to survive in college can differ. Growing up, we hear of fraternities, sororities, and college parties. While the US media platforms show us the fun and social life, the reality is much different, and much more is involved in a college experience.

US News[49] lists some of the main things to conceptualize and understand when thinking of going into a US college. Regardless of if you are an international or a US student, some of the main things to consider when entering college are what it will be like in college, student life / social life, deciding a major, your classes, and professors. These are the main factors in college to consider because you will encounter these factors

---

49 "What to Know about the US College Experience Before Applying," US News, 2014, accessed January 13, 2017, http://www.usnews.com/education/blogs/international-student-counsel/2014/09/09/what-to-know-about-the-us-college-experience-before-applying.

at some point in college.

College life, as the US News describes it, is really like a full-time job. When you go to college, you are an adult, and you are given much information in a very short period. Chances are you are living on campus, in a dorm provided by your campus, or you are traveling from home to your school. The next four or more years in college will be spent mainly on-campus—everything from your academics, breakfast, lunch, and dinner to your social life. After you are done with your orientation, you are pretty much on your own. You are responsible for everything you do and all the choices you make. Yes, you can pick out your classes and the timing to fit your schedule, but regardless of it will still feel like you are in college the whole day. You are most likely running class to class or having a short break where you get very little social time and most likely in the library or a quiet study area to take a nap or study. The college experience catches up to you if you take it slow in the beginning. The experience is intense from the moment you have your orientation, and you are on your way registering for classes, picking out class sections based on the professor's review, and somehow matching it with your already packed schedule.

The classes are intense because you are required to go to class every day, sit in class for hours, take notes, focus on the material, and after your day of classes, go home or go to your dorm to review all your notes. Chances are, after a long day of classes, you are knocked out after you get home or in your dorm and take care of whatever you need to do. Aside from that, there is always the late-nighter you go through, especially before every exam or assignment, emphasizing the midterm and finals time in your four months of the semester. This is pretty much the overall everyday experience of a full-time student.

The intensity is quite a bit, and it catches up to you and can take a toll on your body. It may seem you do not get too many assignments as you used to throughout the end of high school, but what you will realize quickly is that though you may only have assignments now and then, they catch up to you, especially when you see the amount of work piled up when you combine all your class assignments.

Your college experience should not be all about academics. If it is, change it. There are many opportunities to get involved with your college student life and get extracurricular activities under your belt and resume. The student life is all the clubs, organizations, and associations on campus. Besides your academics, you should think about getting involved in the student life in your college, whether it be a club associated with your major, a club of interest, student government, or a social movement/cause in your college. There will always be new things popping up in your college. These activities are great ways to find yourself in your adulthood and college and know who you are and what you are about aside from your major. If you do not have a passion or still not sure what to major in, this is a great way to find yourself and choose a major. By being involved in the student life at your campus and being a student leader of the campus, other opportunities may come your way as well.

Another factor impacting your college experience is deciding your major. Deciding on a major is a key factor because it transforms you into whom you become by graduating on a professional and personal level. A major should not just be chosen suddenly. There is a reason college gives you your first two years in college to take your general education requirements before choosing your major. Use this time to find yourself and know yourself. You choose a major that should follow you throughout your life if you know yourself and your passion. What some students may do is test out different majors throughout their time in college. Students may change their major just because it becomes a little too hard or realize this is not what they want to do their whole lives. The best advice I gave anyone during my college life and my student leadership days is to be passionate about what you do to the point where your major is like a legal and good drug because of the fulfillment you have by serving in the major you are in.

Some students may not know what that means and what it entails when choosing a major. When I say to choose a major that is like a drug to you, and you are passionate about, treat it as if finance was not a major factor in any job you have, you would do something in your major for free as if you are volunteering and not getting paid for it. Throughout your life, certain things make you think about who you are and make you evaluate yourself. These are times that can make someone know themselves. What that leads to is knowing yourself and knowing your passion. If you have that secured in your life, choosing a major should not be a problem.

The last major factor in college is going to your classes and meeting your professors, which can be interesting and fun experiences, or your time to sleep in the boring classes. The classes are divided by the departments that divide the classes into sections to put a random professor in the class to teach. Many of these professors are either actual professors of the college working full time or adjuncts who can work in multiple colleges. The professors determine if you will stay in the class after the first week or change to another section. Most professors will follow your simple one test every month as well as the midterm and final. You may be taking about three to five exams, including the midterm and final. The professors will also give you in-class and homework assignments and papers. The grade breakdown in your syllabus shows the grade percentage breakdown. It shows you how many percentages of tests and assignments or projects/papers go towards your final grade. Among all your professors that you will ever meet in your college tenure, there will be those who are fair and have a well-balanced breakdown of grades that count toward your final grade and those who have a ridiculous percentage breakdown of grades.

Your professors are ultimately there to be there for you and help you along the way in the class as much as possible. They have office hours that you should use very wisely if they fit into your schedule. Some professors are there to give grades and teach the class. The challenging professors might give you a hard time and have no leeway or flexibility. The professor you choose is crucial. Luckily for students, there are the well-known resources of Rate My Professor and your friends who can give you advice on what class to take and what professor to take it with. Use these forms of resources whenever you are applying for classes. It can help you and may even be a big factor in getting that A+.

The first-year experience in college consists of anticipation, anxiety, and discoveries.[50] You are no longer in high school, and you are about to enter the hell of your education. College in any year during your time there is the most stressful and intense time of your life. Your first year lays the foundation for the next four years, or however, much longer you will be in college. You will

---

50 "The First Year College Experience," Campus Life, November 30, 1999, accessed January 13, 2017, http://www.collegeconfidential.com/first-year/.

notice the amount of workload, which will catch you off guard. Not knowing how to study on a college level, you may try to study as you did in high school. If studying and memorizing information from class are natural to you, then you are set. You should see how long what you have been doing works for you. After that first test in one of your classes, it is probably after that will strike you to realize what it takes to study for your classes.

There will be a lot of sacrifices and many things that will change for you. This experience will hit you in one of your difficult classes. Some of the other sacrifices in your first year you will have to make until you are used to college as your social life. If you think you will continue with the same social circle as you did in high school or spend as much time with your social life as you did in high school, you are wrong. Whether it be your social life, family gatherings, or just friends, most things will change if you succeed in college. The academics will take up most of your time, and you will not know what hit you when grades start pouring in.

The first year of college will make you realize you are on your own twenty-four hours a day. There is no one to do anything for you. Every decision and every friend you make will all be on you. This also does not mean you have to change. The positive side of the college is that it is not full of immature kids like in high school. You and your peers are all grown adults thinking about your future and your academics to make something out of yourself. Whether it be a religious organization, a club you are in, or a classmate you meet in your first year, everything plays a role in the person you are to become when you finish college, and it all starts from your first semester in college.

Some of the major challenges during your time in college

are tackling your classes, your professor's grading system, and the administration when they do not play in your favor or give you a hard time. Naturally, classes are divided by credits, and the more credits the class has, the harder it is. However, no matter what, give equal importance to all your classes. A strategy full-time students use to balance their classes is taking two hard classes and two easy classes. It will be obvious which are easy and hard classes when you are registering for your classes. Usually, the math and sciences are the hardstand; they happen to have four credits usually. Other classes could be an elective course or a class for your major, including the math and science classes you might be taking. The trick is to prioritize and a little extra time with your math and science and all your other extra hard courses. They can get very difficult regardless, and there is no guarantee of an A or A+. However, try to make sure there is a well-balanced grading system in your classes and do all your work. Therefore, even if you do not do that great in the tests, your assignments and participation will determine a part of your grade.

As far as your professors are concerned, make sure they know you. Students involved in their classes and participated, the professors will know you; and when it comes to your academics, they may be able to help you out with whatever is available and allowed. I am not saying they will play favoritism with you, but they will understand your situation if you are trying hard but have a difficult time in the classroom. These are things you will also hear during your orientation or from others that are college veterans. Professors are your biggest source during your time in that class, and if you are lucky to get to know them much longer, they can be very helpful in the future.

Some professors have ridiculous grading systems that

may teach well, but the class system in that situation is just not going to be in your favor. There are professors of all kinds, those who have a balanced grading system, those who do not even use testing as part of grading, and those who have unimaginable grading. I have experienced it all. I had some of the best professors that used the portfolio education system to grade us, and I aced in the class. I also had professors that had 60–100 percentage just for tests on the grading rubric. It is professors like those who have unrealistic grading rubrics that need to reevaluate their grading. Furthermore, professors should not be allowed to change their grading rubric in the middle of the semester. Therefore, expect all forms of professors but use resources that are available to pick out your professors.

The administration in the colleges consists of the admissions office, office of student activities, registrar's office, testing office, bursar, and financial aid office. Some of the major issues students face are in the bursar and financial aid office. There seem always to be students facing some forms of problems with financial aid and bursar. The system in this cannot change in terms of the work the staff in the office does, but they can avoid things. Students are from time to time surprised or shocked to see their tuition. From time to time, we may hear of unrealistic tuition that a student may not know where it came from. Anything regarding financial aid and bursar seems to be issues of timing of getting things done. The staff in these offices need to work diligently and on time. The timing of these financial transactions impacts what students may face. Things such as working within a manageable time and solving the issues students face are the responsibility the financial aid and bursar's office staff face. They should be well-trained and well-informed of the issues that can arise and the timing to fix those issues. As a student, stay updated with your tuition and be aware of what is due when. Make sure you take the time to pay off what needs to be paid and do what needs to be done. Do not wait last minute to do things.

The administrative offices are misinforming student's major problem with the other administrative offices mentioned. What happens is that students are given the runaround from time to time without any clear information of their situation. If a student is facing an issue, the administrative staff should tell them which office to go to. It is only during the common questions that they can tell where to go. Whenever a student faces a unique and possibly an unusual issue, the administrative staff should hear out the full issue and properly guide the student to the right office based on the situation. What the student may immediately hear is to go to another office. Students should be given more time, especially during unique and difficult situations. The administrative staff is there to help and resolve the problems students face. Therefore, the student's experience with the administrative staff should be as such, so they feel they are there to help and value the issue someone faces.

The way to make the best out of your college experience is through a balance between your academics, studying, social life, and club/student leadership involvement. The academics and studying for your classes are your set priority. Therefore, treat them as such. You are going to hear of multiple studying methods to keep up with your academics. Honestly, there is no set way to study. Just do what works for you. Every course is different and is going to need equal timing and equal importance. However, one thing to do is try to get all your classes done within a set number of days. If you are willing to stay in school from morning to night, choose to do it carefully. You may also want to spread out your classes by the number of days needed to go to school. A suggestion would be to try to have your classes in three to four days. One of the things that many people do is have classes from Monday to Thursday and have Friday to Sunday off. Whatever you choose, there are ups and downs for all strategies. Choose what works best for you based on your daily life schedule.

The social life in your college depends on several factors, and the experience you get out of it is very enriching and enjoyable. Your social circle and people you are with on a daily to weekly basis relieve your stress from your academics. Each person's experience is different. It is no longer like high school, where it may be hard to break the ice between people. Starting as a freshman, you are in a class full of freshmen in the same classroom. Breaking the ice may take a few weeks or a mere one-classroom session. The social college life depends on you and your personality. There are no social expectations or special groups or specific types of people who have their crowd like in high school. Meeting new people is much easier, and you will be doing it quite frequently.

Social college life is all about where you are and whom you see daily, and the things you and your friends choose to do in your free time.[51] You are in college, and the last thing you need is constant academic stress. Therefore, get involved in your college and hang out with your friends. Find people similar to you and get to know them. Do not miss out on the opportunities of hanging out. It is a great way to get your mind off your academics and relax for a while. Whatever year of

---

51 "Students Speak: What College Social Life Is Really Like," College Board, 2017, accessed January 13, 2017, https://bigfuture.collegeboard.org/find-colleges/campus-life/students-speak-what-college-social-life-is-really-like.

college you are in, your student life will always include your academics, your social life with your friends, and student leadership opportunities if you choose to be involved in it.

Student leadership is a major part of every college and part of the student's life in college. As a college student, you have the opportunity to make a difference and get involved in your school community. The student life and student leadership may start with you as a club member you enjoy. When you get involved in a club and stay there for the long term, work your way up work your way up and run in elections, your club holds elections for the executive board. If you can become involved in the club as an officer, some opportunities may come for you. Not only will you be noticed by your club or program, but there are special trips or opportunities you can be involved in that may arise. Being a student leader of the college lets you participate and impact the community you cater to, and you get to make a difference. From there, you may be involved in something bigger, like becoming an officer in your college's student government. It is these forms of opportunities and much more that make the college experience worth having and enjoyable. Whether it be a club, organization, student government, or something you are doing to help your college community get involved.

Furthermore, during your time in college, you should always try to know the administrative officials in your college. This may be much harder in a four-year college than a community college. Especially if you are in a special program, you should know the administrative staff and make sure they know you. They then become your resources, and that is what they are there for. The administrative staff in your colleges are there to guide you and help you. There will always be certain students that stand out in their minds. Make a good first impression and try to be involved and help out in any way you can. Sooner or later, they will know who you are by name, and you can have a professional and personal relationship during your time in college and possibly even long past that.

By implementing this advice, you get to know your college and university for what they are. There is probably a motto they live by, and unless you experience your college in all avenues, you will not understand how your college differs from others or what is special about your college. Ultimately what you are doing is trying to find the balance between a college education and a social life in college while maintaining satisfactory grades and a satisfactory GPA. Being involved in one side too much more than the other can take a toll on your body, making you feel like your education is not worth it. It is up to you how you choose to spend your college days and balance every part of a college experience. Therefore, whether it be your academics, social circle, clubs, or student life in your college, you make your experience by being involved and by using the resources available to make it the best experience possible for you.

Customized Education

Education itself is a system that students are privileged to be in to become educated and knowledgeable about everything worldwide. Through it, the purpose of education is to choose a field of study during your higher education and dedicate a lifetime of career to the field or multiple fields during your work tenure. Through this process, everyone that obtains an education goes through the same process of elementary, intermediate, high school, and college. Furthermore, if you choose to go for even higher studies or if you are required to, you look to obtain your master's or Ph.D. By being part of US education, you are told what to take every year of your schooling.

Furthermore, even when you are in college, you are told to take certain classes for your major and general education requirements. That leaves you with a choice of freely choosing the classes to take for any elective courses you take. This system fails to consider the difficulties students can face if everyone is told what to take, with little room for freely choosing what to take. The system requires change that can work for everyone through a customized education.

The US education system is based on schooling and standardized testing for intelligence on different subjects to obtain a GPA. Through that, it is supposed to be a reflection of what you know. The US education currently is a lot like living in a box without any real say or flexibility. We are all within a system of what we are supposed to learn and study. Therefore, we are then in a governing system that trickles down from the state government down to the hands of the teachers that tell us. For many broader policies and agendas, the system trickles down from the federal government. We are governed by people who think they understand how students learn or what works best. There are things like the learning system of the education system (i.e., testing) that come from the federal government. We as a nation—unless we change and give students the complete freedom of deciding what to learn and what classes to take—are stuck in a system that does not reflect the full potential or knowledge of students and their capabilities. If we are stuck with standardized testing our entire life, our grades have no value.

Therefore, what we are going through right now devalues our intellect and the creativity and true understanding of what is taught to us. We can only keep so much information in our brains, especially when it comes to testing. There is only a certain amount of information we can keep in mind, and we are required to give these tests based on it within the time we study for the tests. Therefore, we are in a failing system that only works for the top 5 percent or the geniuses for studying and memorizing information work. However, we need to be in an education system where we are not required to memorize information to try to be successful in tests, but in a system where we can showcase our true understanding and intellect—as well as not be forced to take the course we know, we cannot be successful in. However, with that, there are two ways to go about it.

A customized education consists of two parts—freedom to choose what classes to take and what not to take and an education system free of standardized testing and implementing a reimagined portfolio that works and does not fail like the past. Starting with the freedom to choose what classes to take, we must first determine where this customized education starts. I believe that it should start in high school. When you are in elementary and middle school, you are usually required to take the common core and possibly one extra class and physical education. Therefore, it is not much of a hassle because you are still learning your grade level basics in the common core. Therefore, your biggest challenge and focus is just the common core. However, when you are in high school, there is much more pressure for different forms of extracurricular activities or different classes to be taken along with a shop class. The classes you take will also depend on the type of high school you go to and the purpose.

There are high schools where it follows the regular classes high school students take, and then there are high schools that are career-oriented, almost like combining a trade school with a high school. Therefore, when you are in high school, the number of classes you have to take varies and can be all over the place. It is not your English, math, science, and social studies / political science classes only. Therefore, my belief is the customized education starts in high school. If you are required to take all these extra courses and are not good at them or have no interest in taking them, why would you ever be forced to take them? I believe having the freedom to choose the extra classes comes into a student's life in high school. They should be optional for the student.

However, the way to go about it can also be debated. In the beginning, if a class sounds interesting and hearing the course description of the class, you should try out the class for a while to see how you do in the class. The student should be able to evaluate if he is personally fit to take the class. The student should be given at least half the semester to see how he does in those extra courses before making the final decision of sticking with the course and having it reflected in his report cards. If he feels he has no interest in the class or is not doing well and cannot keep up with his classmates, he can choose to opt-out of the class. After determining his permanent schedule, determine the number of credits the student is required to take to graduate high school.

The second part of how to make this customized education even better is shutting down standardized testing and implementing the portfolio education system. If the standardized testing still exists, the education system will still be bittersweet. On one hand, we would get the freedom to choose what class to take and what not to take; however, we would be stuck with a testing system that we know does not work. Of course, I have already touched on the issue with the current standardized testing in the first chapter. Therefore, refer to the first chapter to refresh yourself with the portfolio education system and the issue with the current standardized testing if needed. We need to implement the portfolio education system and change any issues we had in the past and test out the new form of the system to see its efficiency.

In college, we are faced with a similar problem and have to implement the same education policy if we can go about changing the education system. Education in college is a little different, being that students are required to take their courses for their major, general education requirements, and elective courses to fulfill 120 credits for a bachelor's degree. Let us first look at the classes to take for your major if we are to break this down. A college education tells us what courses we can take. It may even be categorized into broader topics. So there may be multiple courses categorized for you to take in a certain category. Therefore, in that case, you have the freedom to choose which course to take that you feel fit in and that may be of interest to you. However, there are times, and there are specified courses that emphasize that major that you must take. The issue lies there.

If we tell students, "These are the main courses for the major, and you have to take it," the value of the education system immediately diminishes. It may be that it does not diminish the value of the major, but then again, we see this entrapment in being forced to take a course. Furthermore, there are these forms of highly emphasized courses and are a must to take for every student regardless of what major they choose to be in. Therefore, in this case, we should choose students to test out or choose if they must take the course. Within one of those courses, a student has a highly difficult time in that form of a subject or learning that material.

An example would be taking statistics as a psychology major even though you are not good at math. Even though there is a huge difference between math and statistics, it still falls in the same category of learning as far as types of subjects are considered. In this case, if a student already knows he is not good at a specific type of subject and medical records are not enough to prove his inefficiency or lack of satisfactory work, he should not be forced to take the course. Later in his career, he should be assisted or choose to do something. He is not required to do statistics in his field, or he can certainly get assistance during his career.

The lack of understanding of a subject should not prevent someone from completely not choosing that field as his/her major. If someone is truly passionate about the field, he should still pursue it, but in the future of his career, he would either be getting assisted or not be doing that specific thing he has had trouble with, and he has not been able to overcome. Nevertheless, once again, we are to give complete control and freedom to the student to choose to take the course or not when he is required to take it. He can also understand it much later in life when he goes for his master's/PhD.

When it comes to the general education requirements, some courses need to be fulfilled, and it is not just the common core we are used to. When it comes to this, the same repeating pattern of issue exists where we are trapped in a system and are told what to take. Only this time, there may be various courses to fulfill the category or type of class. However, the common courses we are used to seeing never leave us. Many new other advanced courses among English, math, science and political science still exist. Depending on person-to-person, they may be good at certain subjects, and they may not be good at another. However, everyone must take some variation of it, which needs to change in our education system. Once again, we are forcing students to take a subject course regardless of if they are good at it or not. The difficulty level for someone to take these courses varies person-to-person. You can put the difficulty range in a spectrum. This issue is highly concerning for those on the far end of extreme difficulty or anything close to it.

These types of students—and really everyone—should have this freedom and choice of choosing what course to take. Furthermore, if they are not willing to take the course due to their extremely high level of difficulty with proof from the past in similar subjects, they should not have to and be opted out of the course but given credit for it. If it is a course or subject, they have no possible way of doing above average, then they should be opted out and given credit so they can move on with their lives and focus on the courses they have to take.

If we are to go back at looking at the ultimate purpose of education, as mentioned in the beginning of the chapter, we see that it is to have a career and a job. However, the issue in our job market in the United States currently is that the value of a GPA does not even hold that big of a value anymore. Employers rather want to see a person have experience in their field and know their job duties. As the saying goes, experience is the best teacher. What you actually know is not determined by your grades in school or your GPA. It is only a mere reflection of a small percentage of your full potential and understanding. Your hands-on experience and understanding are what will prove your worth for your job and career.

Furthermore, these days, a simple bachelor's degree is not enough to obtain a job in most fields. Many people might say the bachelor's degree today is equivalent to a high school degree for most fields of study, and a master's degree is a bachelor's degree these days. Therefore, most fields require a master's degree. All these degrees may have no value if you do not get anything out of them. You get a paper with your name and degree name on it. Therefore, if we do not reform the education system for what it can be and learn to our full potential, the customized education is an option to implement for our education even to have value truly.

The US education system is in a rut where students are just inside a governed system and are told what to study and what classes to take. The reform here I speak of is a system where all students can have the complete freedom and choice to their education. I am asking to implement a customized education for students from high school. Students are just stuck with classes they are told to take, and they have very little say what class to take. We do not see this full complete choice of freedom to an extent until students are in college. Students are taking their common core all throughout elementary and middle school, with an extra class or two in middle school. However, that completely changes from high school where there are extra courses to take like shop classes that students may not be completely comfortable with. From there in college, we see a completely different form of classes to take aside the general education requirements, which include the common core.

The college curriculum is a little different since you are required to take general education courses, your courses for your major, and elective courses, which are really the only complete freedom you have in choosing what to take. What I proposed is to be allowed to choose what courses you have to take from your general education requirements. Your major may have multiple choices for a category of classes that you can choose from, but that flexibility is not completely there for your general education requirements. Your college may divide up your general education courses to sections and let you choose courses from there. However, there are certain general education and major courses that you are forced to take. There are obviously always the advanced courses for your common core and major that you are required to take. Then there are courses that are just mandatory courses for your major. However, it is these same courses that may be similar to a common core like statistics and math that you are mandated to take as a psychology major. However, these one or two courses should not stop you from choosing that major. Having the complete freedom to test the waters in those courses and choosing if you want to take those courses or not should be in complete control of the student.

As with any class or course, your grades are a mere reflection of your potential, and therefore, if we are stuck with standardized testing rather than changing to the portfolio education system, we should be equipped with a customized education to the student's liking for the best academic outcome possible. The job market looks at experience and knowledge and skills pertaining to the job and field. Maybe, if we had a more valid education system, our true knowledge and potential would reflect our grades.

The Future of the U.S. Education System

The future of US education is uncertain. With all the issues mentioned in the context of this book and all the stories and issues you are about to read from other students, the education system is in jeopardy. Many of these issues are just there, and there may be things done here and there. However, some issues like standardized testing and bullying are global issues that may remain here forever or at least to the twenty-second generation when the kids of the twenty-first generation have all grown up, and many of them will be in executive power just like our current government is. The future is quite unclear and requires change.

We are in a generation where the kids and young adults of the twenty-first generation are the mainstays of the generation, and with it, we lead the movements in anything regarding our education system. There are many forms of advocacy and many things that our state governments hear. However, there is a bigger issue in all of this to ensure the proper education system and proper teaching methods to be implemented during our time and the future generations. There are major issues like the issues discussed in part one of the books with little hopes and sparks whenever a story hits the media. However, it should not be that we have to rely on stories to make it to the news for students, parents, educators, and education advocates to react and start a protest or rally to see change. We have been voicing on and asking for change, but there seems to be no major impact or change.

We are still stuck with a testing system that fails the US education system and its students and still stuck with students getting bullied every day of their school lives. Our US education system has also taken a turn for its worst after 9/11, and its Muslim students and other minorities may not be the same as others are getting affected every day. With how the US education system is going, there is a future that I fear for current students and for the students to come in future generations. Students may have the right to an education; however, they are stuck in an unfair system. For these students, their full potential may not be seen or even heard of or acknowledged. There is no insurance policy for the success parents and students hope for and dream of and the idea they have of the American Dream. It is not until students are in the system and face the harsh reality of how the US education system sees the issues stopping them from their true potential and success.

Nevertheless, there are always miracle stories we hear of, and automatically our mind switches to the idea that if one person can do it, everyone can. However, that is simply a delusional mindset to have because it is not reality. As much as it may be a way to motivate someone, it is not how it works out for students. Students face way too many abstract obstacles within the US education system and outside with the personal life issues they go through. Every student is different, and every student's situation is different.

Students come from all different backgrounds and families, as well as different abilities and disabilities. However, through it all, there are certain things that all students face or cross paths with at some point in their education, whether it be the administration, financial issues, college life, and issues there, or any other issues. Certain things are the same, and certain things can be changed. The education system and the way we choose to teach our kids and test their intelligence remain constant. It is up to the state and federal governments and the board of education to look forward and be the change everyone, hopes for.

Without the changes or hearing out what our students, parents, teachers, and education advocates want to ensure the success of our students, we as a nation will remain stale and fall behind with our fellow education systems overseas. We also have to understand and most likely explain to the past generations (especially those that bring a lot of their homeland mindset and base things off that) that there is more to an education system than the simple schooling students go through. There are beliefs and expectations students have from their parents that do not simply work out for them. We are also in a system where there is an entire government and people in power that sit in offices at our state capitals that tell how things are supposed to be. There is an entire system that is not in favor of the students and is simply there for the money and the policies they alone feel are right. People have gone far too long speaking out, and not enough has been going on, and no major changes have gone on aside from a few.

Some of the biggest issues have been voiced, and yet, we

are still stuck with a system where those issues are not resolved and changed. This is where there is a need for global change within the nation. We are when the government has become the students, and the students have become the government. Well, at least, that is how it should be. The US government is offering students a free public education and is supposed to cater to us. However, if they do not hear our voices and the changes required, what value does our education hold?

As much as we can learn everything about this world and are given a ton of knowledge about various fields, the end goal does not meet the standards outlined in our US education system. Our grades and knowledge do not tell the whole story of what students go through to get what they got. Furthermore, it is not fair for how we obtained it and what we had to go through to obtain our grades. When all is set and done, it is our grades that give a reflection of our effort and education, but honestly, it is an abstract thing that cannot be tested for every student because everyone has had their struggles and put in their efforts to do the best they possibly can. However, it does not tell us an equal chance to be truly successful in our classes and our grades. Schooling ultimately revolves around our grades, and it is what every student does not have—the ultimate equal chance of showing their full potential and understanding for a grade even to be labeled on the students.

As mentioned earlier, the students have become the government, and the government has become the students. We are now in a system that does not work for students, and our government is not listening to the millions of voices that speak out to make changes in our testing system of all things, first, the global issue of bullying and many other things. We still see the same issues come up, and in many cases, the issues take a turn for their worst and cause death and suicide, among many other things. The system seems to tend to individual cases aside from a few movements and policies signed into law or passed over the years. However, how much does it change to help everyone out? Shouldn't there be certain things and certain issues that need to be nationwide and dealt with it as outlined in a way that works?

We are still relying on the government to do things because of their power; however, it is only from time to time that we hear of something. For example, issues like standardized testing and bullying need the voices and knowledge of educators, parents, and, most importantly, the students to lay out an agreed-upon and tested plan, and, ultimately, that works. If we remain as we are currently and the changes, we ask for are not heard and provided, we should question our government about the value of our education system. It is no longer about which neighborhood has the best schools or where to get the best education. It is about how we, as a nation, can make a global change to give every student an equal opportunity for academic success.

Our voices and concerns are not something that can be taken lightly, and it is a time where what we say goes. It is no longer about how our government wants things to be. We are the students going through the US education system, and it is us that are affected by the system. If our voices and issues are not given priority, what do we gain from everything we do? We need an education reform that works for every student regardless of race, religion, background, ability, disability, and most importantly, understanding and knowledge or lack of. As much as we have the right to an education, we should have an equal opportunity to succeed in our education system.

What I hope to see through this book and the future of US education is for those in power to understand the issues our students, parents, teachers, and education advocates speak of and make the changes that are possible, starting with eliminating standardized testing and implementing a reimagined portfolio education system that was spoken of in this book or take suggestions from the people to implement a system that works. Every issue mentioned in this book should be looked at with an open mind and see what is feasible and what can be done to change a reality. Even if we cannot change the issues to be exactly how it has been outlined in this book, we, as a nation, have to get as close to it as possible. We can no longer accept a system that does not work. The students have truly become the government of the education system, and the government has become the students of the education system. However, our government now needs to listen to the student's voices and make the changes we need.

Part II

Voices of the System

Education's Purpose

Corrina Blau

One of the most difficult obstacles school reformers face is establishing the true purpose of education. Aside from keeping children out of the labor force and providing free childcare to working parents, reformers have to recognize the true purpose of schools—to cultivate the natural curiosity and desire for productivity that all people are born with. From the first day I entered the New York public school system fourteen years ago; I was subjected to a deprivation of play, test-based curriculums, underpaid teachers, and a bureaucracy that dehumanizes all involved. These rigid practices restrict freedom of thought and expression, deprive student's agency to study what they please, and are detrimental to the health and well-being of students and teachers. Our school system is so broken that 40–50 percent of teachers leave within their first five years of teaching, costing the country billions of dollars each year. If it were not for the grace of a few amazing teachers, I might have spent my whole life believing that education is a punitive, unhappy ordeal. Luckily, I discovered that true education is the exposure to fascinating new ideas, crucial information about our society, and a guide in how to relate to other people. Truly learning is not rote memorization. It is the euphoric process of understanding an unintelligible and unknowable world just a little bit better. In the mess that is American public schools, I found glimmers of the true meaning of education, and for that, I am eternally grateful. The object of all school reformers should be to expand these lucky, sparse experiences into a model for how all schools should operate all the time. I began public school full-time at the age of five when I entered kindergarten. We were expected to sit relatively still for six hours a day, complete homework each night, and rarely ventured outdoors. The hour of free play we were allotted each day mysteriously disappeared when we entered first grade. I strongly believe that young students can only learn by playing and that adults play by learning new things. At that time, these two activities were very much separated. I do not have particularly strong memories of these first few years. Our classrooms were usually about twenty-five students to one teacher, with a paraprofessional on occasion. I believe the social interactions with my peers were more relevant to my development than the phonics books we utilized or the handwriting we practiced. My teachers were generally overworked, but some of them were very nurturing. There was much pressure to focus. I can remember three separate occasions in which teachers asked me kindly to stop staring out the window. As a babysitter and a tutor, I can certainly appreciate the urge to have students *pay attention* and stare at their notebooks, the chalkboard, and the teacher's face. Unfortunately, the expectation that young children can sit still and focus for so long is just unrealistic. If we truly want to reform education, we will have to accept that staring at moving clouds, falling snowflakes, or any other distracting scene might be more interesting and relevant to a kid than the PowerPoint at the front of the classroom. By far, the highlight of each day was the 3:00 pm dismissal bell, when I could finally run around in the park with my friends.

Although academic assessments began in kindergarten, state testing did not commence until third grade. The disparity of resources in schools across the country and even within different neighborhoods in New York is extreme, so having national standards is not in and of itself a bad thing. The issue is the degree to which teachers are judged based on their student's test scores. Test scores even influence the amount of funding a school gets. Underperforming students can be held back a year, and their teachers could be fired; this is ludicrous; a teacher alone cannot be held responsible for some arbitrary test grade when the home environment and educational background of students ranges so much. Unfortunately, the effects of this ladder of pressure are very real. I cannot emphasize enough how much of my education was dedicated to test prep. Teachers were instructed to show us how to narrow down multiple choice answers and form cookie-cutter short answers. The biggest controversy among teachers was whether we should listen to the read-aloud test passages once and then take notes or whether we should take notes both times. To add insult to injury, the passages were almost always tedious non-fiction pieces about children our age whom a test creator somewhere believed would be relatable. The ordeal was extensive and mind-numbingly boring, and it did not resemble any version of true education. It was pseudo-learning.

In a way, I was lucky. Most of my teachers could not hide the bureaucracy-induced disdain they felt drilling us on test-taking skills, and my parents made it clear that my worth as a person was not solely dependent on getting a grade of 4, 3, or heaven forbid a 2. However, the message I received as a child was that a school is a place where time is wasted, boredom is suffered, and no one in my actual school controls what we learn (or do not learn).

Teachers are as many victims of bad school systems as students are. Although the median salary for all public school teachers is $56,000 a year, the starting salary for all teachers is only $37,000. The implication is that public school teachers are neither valued nor considered professionals. Low salary is partly responsible for low retention rates, but a lack of control is also a reason teachers transfer schools or leave the profession altogether. A more enlightened English teacher once told me that his curriculum book instructed him on what to say to his class and how to say it, and where to stand when he did. He was one of my best teachers because he ignored these hyper rationalizations and talked to us like we were people, standing wherever he pleased.

Looking back on the incredible range of teachers I have witnessed from the first moment I entered kindergarten to my second year in a public university, I am baffled by the lack of oversight teachers receive. Indeed, the test scores teachers produce are harshly scrutinized, but how they interact with their students seems irrelevant. Unfortunately, this leaves students vulnerable to some truly unprofessional and incapable teachers. A 2014 video of an elementary school teacher at Success Academy charter school berating a first grader for stumbling on a math problem recently went viral. The video exposed teaching practices at the charter school that was borderline abusive. Students were publicly humiliated for making small academic mistakes, failing to pay attention, or playing with toys in class. Parents of children who had been or still attend Success

Academy later reported the extreme symptoms of stress their children routinely experienced, including bed-wetting, crying in class, and vomiting on exam papers.

These stories resonated strongly with my experience in public elementary school in the early 2000s. Teachers would use humiliation to control students, and it became clear that making mistakes was not a useful aspect of my education. One elementary school substitute teacher would line up all her students and embarrass those who could not answer in their heads the math problems she asked. A seventh-grade Spanish teacher would do the same with a *Jeopardy!* game that became a weekly nightmare. The next year, a math teacher would repeatedly call out the same kids to answer algebra problems, and when they inevitably answered incorrectly, he would embarrass them in the same way. The culminating lesson from all these examples was that any wrong answer was extremely shameful. Children do not have the language skills to insist on using a pen and paper to work out the problem. They cannot advocate for their right to learn through practice and experimentation. With teacher observations being as rare as they were, students are vulnerable to a minority of teachers who are—quite frankly—assholes.

After so many poor experiences in the public school system, I am eternally grateful to the teachers who showed me the true meaning of education. I was lucky enough to attend a more progressive arts-based high school, and I met teachers who were caring, brilliant, and in some ways life-changing. Many of my teachers seemed genuinely interested in their student's opinions and our thought process overall. One of my favorite history teachers would insist we play devil's advocate on every issue, no matter how strongly we *did not* disagree. In high school, I was able to take advanced placement courses that were rigorous but extremely enjoyable, and I completed a behavioral science Intel project with the help of several dedicated advisers. It did not win the national Intel competition (or even come close to placing), but my appreciation for the intrinsic value of education had been solidified by this time. I had teachers who were offbeat and eccentric, and every extended deadline and forgiven late homework assignment reinforced a new idea—education for the sake of education. Students respond well to teachers who care about academia in its purest form. For all their bluster about counting down until the last day of school and the beginning of that precious paid summer vacation, I truly believe they wanted to be there.

If the United States does not change the way schools operate, the results will be insidious. Young students will continue to suffer extreme stress based on inconsequential assignments, over-testing, and overworked teachers. Teachers will continue to leave schools at alarming rates, and unfortunately, the scourge that is charter schools will spread even more. Many charter schools do not support teachers' unions and select bright kids from poor neighborhoods in a way that depletes local public schools. The school system is already so unequal, with wealthy neighborhoods supporting local public schools through fund-raising, taxes, and active parent-teacher associations in a manner that poorer neighborhoods could not possibly compete with. In an ideal world, the United States would have to mimic several other countries' successful practices to achieve comparable results. For example, Finland is ranked as the best education system globally, but they have abolished private schooling. This means that rich people have an incentive to make sure public schools are adequate for their children (and thus, all children). As amazing as this would be for the United States, abolishing private schools and religious schools would not be constitutional. Many European countries limit the amount of time spent in school daily, especially for younger kids. Finnish kids do not begin regular school until the age of seven. Again, the cost for American parents to keep their young kids in school only twenty hours a week would be astronomical. Many ideal changes to our school system are impossible because our society would have to change drastically to allow it. The emphasis on extreme work weeks, consumerism, and quantifiable results would have to be replaced by a code of humanitarianism and an emphasis on overall well-being.

There are aspects of change that truly are feasible for the United States. Teachers starting should not be paid such low wages just because they are new. Teaching is currently the largest occupation in America, so it should be respected. Successful teachers should be the norm, not a rare occurrence. In Japan, teachers routinely go to conferences to compare their teaching methods with peers in their fields. It is important to recognize that teaching is a different skill from any knowledge of a specific discipline. A chemist could be amazing at chemistry but still cannot explain the basics of their field to an introductory class. The teacher-student ratio also needs to change. In the United Kingdom, most primary schools have a one-to-ten teacher-student ratio. Even if two of the three teachers in the classroom are assistants, their support is crucial. Finally, state testing should be used for informational purposes only. Underperforming schools should not be penalized or shut down. They should be offered more resources to help their students. Teachers also need to drastically reduce the amount of homework they give to primary school students. Homework has not been shown to improve overall performance, and it makes students and parents alike miserable. Either the direction of education in the United States becomes more progressive, or it does not. It is impossible to predict the future, but the present should be considered a crisis mode, and I know that if the system remains, I would be deeply unhappy sending children of my own to public schools.

There is enormous relief in finally beginning to enjoy school after years of declaring one's hatred for it. The cognitive dissonance kids in the United States suffer is intense. We are constantly told how lucky we are to have free and compulsory education, the great equalizer, the cornerstone of our democracy. However, many of us despise it, producing feelings of guilt, laziness, and ingratitude. When I learned that school could be a good place, I was relieved not only for my mental health and future aspirations but also because the claims of education's virtues now made sense. I had discovered the difference between school and education. A school is the building we spend a third of our childhood in. True education is exploring the world in a way that changes one's perspective forever, makes one question everything he/she thought he/she knew, and makes one hopeful. It is a rush of endorphins that fill the recipient with relief and happiness.

Furthermore, it is practical. Education should be about helping people relate better to each other and the world. The goals should be leading healthy and happy lives and becoming productive members of society. Many of the expectations placed on children are detrimental, and the unrelenting boredom and vulnerability they face are unfair. However, I am so thankful that true bits of education still do exist in America. Reformers need to recognize the successes of hardworking teachers, students, and administrators and expand these experiences to encompass all schools. There are tangible practices that need to be altered, such as increasing teacher pay and decreasing school days.

However, the way we look at education as a whole requires the most change. Education does not have to be forced and painful. No one should doubt the inherent desire for productivity that all children harbors. After all, I document my experiences not for any grade or extra credit reward but rather out of a pure intrinsic desire to define what may be indefinable—the true purpose of education.

A Diversified Approach to American Education

Raimondo Graziano

Education is the foundation for an informed, empathetic, and productive citizenry. It is essential for the function of a proper liberal democracy. Now the United States is meant to embody the ideals of liberal democracy. However, we lack so gravely in education; our students are falling far behind the rest of the world in proficiency, comprehension, and applicability. I know from my personal experiences within the halls of the hallowed institution that there is something very wrong. For whatever the reason may be, the prime focus of education is to excel in scores and maximize your human capital. Learning is not the end of *learning.* The sentiment within the American classroom is not "How does this knowledge broaden my understanding of my collective world and the global community?" but rather "How does this knowledge help me progress to the next class, to the next grade, to the next point of perceived self-achievement with minimal work put in?"

This is a broad generalization of the thoughts and feelings within an American classroom but let us be clear. There is a reason why there are perceptions regarding the intelligence of

Americans. General conversation with people will tell you that Americans know very little of the complexity and dynamics of global politics, mathematics, the sciences, and other fields. Moreover, the supposed ignorance of the American people is a topic of discussion abroad. Education has become a twisted precursor to careerism. There is something intrinsically deeper in the process of learning than that of simply landing an occupation to use whatever pennies you have left from your numerous obligations to buy a pair of ripped jeans. America has lost its love of learning.

Moreover, we will only find it if we start with our youth and make learning the priority and testing a nonissue in the early formative years of American education. The United States of America has to face certain realities if we intend to make strides toward educating our students unrivaled by any other nation globally. How the United States approaches, education is centered heavily on testing, involving quizzes, examinations, a large amount of homework, and a focus on what we like to call extracurricular activities. Those sorts of things, of course, take a back seat to the actual curriculum, while for many students, the true love of learning and growth can be attributed to these sorts of activities. There is a connection to it, which informs the degree of learning, whether it be a great deal or completely dismissed by the student. Firstly, the United States must focus on curriculum-based learning and a portfolio system that exhibits student's progress throughout the school year. Secondly, the United States needs to allow more personal freedom and accountability regarding its students and teachers. A student is expected to learn and complete work without question, and for many students, the asinine amount of work does not allow them to build on the foundations that their interests have dictated. If students are inherently against or averse to a particular subject or activity, they ought to opt-out of it when they have sufficient education to function in our society.

This is especially so if students would be benefitted to a greater degree by honing their individual inters. We hear a great deal from our teachers and administrators how the school is our "job" to think of it as a nine-to-five. While they say this, it is not treated as such. Furthermore, education has become laughable and a bore for many students. It does not have the same weight that it is used to carry.

Furthermore, this is evident in our standing internationally. Our students fall far behind other industrialized nations. How can we speak of our exceptionalism when our students and teachers are being shortchanged? Our exceptionalism lies in our hope and our tenacious planning for tomorrow. In order to execute this, I believe that the following needs to occur. Furthermore, though it may be strenuous and met with opposition, the solutions offered now only help exacerbate the problem and add needless bureaucracy to an already muddled system.

The United States education system is left heavily up to the jurisdiction of the states and local counties to dictate based on loose guidelines set forth by the Department of Education on how and what to teach our children. For the United States to remain an effective leader globally, not only in education but in all aspects of our global preeminence, we must consolidate and centralize our government to achieve a greater degree of productivity, efficiency, and unity across state borders. This would mean that the United States would have to extend the school day and the amount of time that is spent in school to effectively teach and prepare students for the rigors of the working world. It is time we treated school as a job comparable to one that garners a wage. A school day starting at 7:00 am and ending at 3:00 pm, with an hour lunch five days a week nationwide. Each student would be provided with the assurance of one week of sick days and one week of personal days. There would be four allotted breaks throughout the year. In the winter and summer, a month off, December and June respectively, and in the fall and spring, a week off, October and April. In this country, there is a separation of church and state inherent in our nation's constitution, so it is just so that these days of religious observance ought to fall under the category of "personal day" and should not affect the education of the remainder of the populace who may be of different religious denominations or none whatsoever. By increasing instruction time, more valuable moments can be had between students and our educators.

Moreover, with a change in the time in school, there comes a change in the way we will administer education. By ensuring that prekindergarten through the eighth grade adheres to the following policy, we embolden and strengthen a stronger and more united foundation for all our American children. No major testing, a comprehensive portfolio for each class with weekly reviews class-wide for understanding and engagement, and a nonpunitive quiz weekly to assess student understanding. Therefore, the students are graded on their work and understanding and are highly discouraged from cheating, as a passing grade on an examination will not be the make-or-break to a school year or class.

These portfolios with comprehensive essays and written assignments complied in class and analysis of theories and expansion of critical thinking in relation to texts and ideas offset the downside of our testing culture. An institution of a no-homework policy, replacing it instead with nightly readings and a summary of said reading as well as yearlong readings of the classics of literature from prekindergarten through the twelfth grade. Beginning in high school, each student will be required to complete a twenty-five-hour trade course yearly to ensure that when students go onward out of school or wherever they may go, they are prepared academically and trained with their hands—something that is disappearing in this world. We have a great deal of respect for technicians and engineers, but the country and our communities still need plumbers, maintenance specialists, and electricians. No job is deserving of being deemed lesser than another.

However, we all understand that schooling not only involves what occurs in the classroom but also our cafeterias, gymnasiums, art departments, general infrastructure, etc. Likewise, we understand that our teachers are often greatly undervalued, but we can recognize that there is a population of teachers that are protected and do not fulfill the obligation and national duty that their occupation entails, which is why being in my belief that the United States ought to do away with tenure and, instead, offer increased pay and incentive bonuses to teachers and educators. This works twofold, rewarding the educators who do their due diligence and making it easier to remove teachers or educators because of misconduct or inattention concerning their profession. We should offer blank assurances to people that breed apathy if the educators in question choose not to fulfill their duties but glide through easily at a second-rate school, disadvantaging the students more so than anyone. While I support unions efforts in securing their workers job security, in a profession as consequential as education, such assurances are irresponsible and impractical, and appropriate measures ought to be taken if there is misconduct of any sort. What must be done is massive investment in our education, but it cannot be looked upon as merely an investment in education but an investment in the future of our country, in our children.

This brings me to perhaps the largest expansion in our American education system that I am proposing. Firstly, the implementation of a community service program starting in prekindergarten through the twelfth grade, beginning at five hours and steadily moving up to seventy-five hours of community service yearly by the end of high school. This service will be done in-house and administered through the Department of Education, ensuring that there is no finagling of information and that the community service and civics courses are adhered to and truly obligatory. To learn is not enough. Our schools and our institutions have the reasonability to help foster children into compassionate, functioning, intelligent, and informed adults whom we would trust with running our government and legislating our lives. The process starts in prekindergarten with a five-hour basic civic course, going up to high school with seventy-five hours completed yearly on top of the trade course. This is to broaden our student's horizons and their potentials and their capacity for work, which is not something that we should avoid—rather, it should be embraced. Secondly, mandate secondary education. However, let me be clear. This does not mean college or university alone. Rather it is the following: Upon completing high school, students can enroll in a four-year program that will allow them to work at a reduced pay rate of $12.75 per hour, coupled with classes in numerous job programs to broaden their skillset and knowledge. However, one of those years is dedicated to compulsory service to either the military or through AmeriCorps. The culmination of this is at the end of four years. These individuals will receive a certificate certified by the Department of Education to be equal in weight to a four-year bachelor's degree. Likewise, those that wish to complete service in the military or to AmeriCorps can enroll in a similar program, yielding the same certificate and job-training classes.

Furthermore, those who wish to serve their country will enroll in a four-year program with the military that will yield this certificate while also instilling education and service in these young men and women. The goal of this expansion is to create the most qualified and informed American electorate and the most civically engaged in our countries history. If implemented, every American by the age of twenty-three will have been enrolled for further education, as well as for those pursuing college or work, one year of service to their country in some form.

This country has an opportunity to do what has not been done before. The United States can effectively create the most informed and engaged citizenry to date. Education for myself has been an integral part of my life for the last thirteen years. All my memories involve the school in some ways.

The school is unequivocally important to the formation of whom we become. Those who are subjected to mediocrity are not always able to overcome and dismiss that very thing. We should strive for excellence and nothing less in something so important when educating the youth and teaching them because it is right, not because we have decided arbitral. They must pass an exam to measure their intellectual capacity. It is then that we become one with our obligations as people—to uplift and offer the best to those that we call our neighbors. This is how we build a foundation for a united and working America.

Civics in Education: An American Approach

Raimondo Graziano

The American way of living is one that is aspired to by many. The masses are attracted to this country because of the idea of this nation more so than the political, social, and economic reality. The United States to this day remains an idea—the idea of which is what we strive for. The idea is what any political group rails and raves for. However, the degree of political apathy present in our nation's streets, universities, and institutions is staggering. While we speak highly of progress and change, little is done to account for the degree of banter. But the blame does not lay solely on the public.

Our institutions and elected officials are failing us. The nature of partisan politics is not an excuse for little to no compromise. The gridlock of our Congress, the division of our people, the misinformation and biased opinions peddled by the media are to blame. And because of this, the public is discontent. While some argue, and push for reform, the vast majority of Americans are concerned with their personal responsibilities. As they should be, but let's stress this here: what is not taught is a sense of duty and purpose to one's country. The problems of our fellow Americans, for the most part, we do not feel are our own. And why would we? Civics and responsibility for one's country and for one's people are not taught or stressed. We deride and tear down the institutions of our government, yet we rarely talk about the good the government does and make the good it can do. We begin to fail the ideals, beliefs, and possibilities of this country when we neglect the youth or when we neglect their education. When the focus becomes the institution and not the citizens living it, we fail the promise of a more prosperous tomorrow.

Education is perhaps the most important pathway for a functional, productive, engaged, and compassionate citizenry. And we are failing to set this standard. We lack and fall far behind our European counterparts across the Atlantic. And we should do well to heed this trend. The youth of the country is who will make the choices and plans for the country when it's their time. So until then, it is our responsibility, not only to the concept of this country but to the people who are the embodiment of such, to work to ensure our education does not fail our students. A collection of national standards for education coupled with an emphasis on the acquisition of knowledge as well as a national civics course can be the defining element in improving educational standards and measures, as well effectively combating political apathy. We need a citizenry that is fiercely active and fervently discusses and debates the issues of our day with every man, woman, and child having their own self-interest as well as their families and neighborhoods pushing them but with a sense that they are striving for the greater idea of the national goals and national good that we can build to.

In short, we need a nation that looks to the words of President John F. Kennedy, "Ask not what your country can do for you, but what you can do for your country." A citizen that is well educated is a citizen that can feed himself/herself. A country that is well educated on the principles of civics is a country that can feed and embolden each other. The idea that we are only as strong as we can be when we are fully united holds true. And education is the foundation on which we can build a unified, nonpartisan, compassionate, and driven country in which we can all share in its bountiful wealth and live up to and surpass the ideals and ideas that keep the brightest minds of the country awake at night. And so the question then becomes "How?" And you need to look no further than your local public school.

My understanding of the public school system comes from my own personal study of it as well as my experience in it for much of my young life. Though I've lived here and many of the opportunities I've been afforded have been *because* of this, that point has never been emphasized really. Ideas of American exceptionalism are tossed aside. And while I can understand this from a point of a globalist need for equality of nations and peoples, I cannot understand why any people would dismiss the idea that they are exceptional and capable of great good. My sense of civic devotion, a pull toward public service and the country, came not from my schooling. It came from my grandparents who were taught by theirs. And I say to those who use that point *against* the need for civic education, who say that government does not need to teach the tenets of good citizenship, and who argue that it's an overstep to keep in mind that a lot of people are not afforded these relationships. And that if a young American cannot be taught his civic duty from those who raise him, it is the responsibility of the state to do so. If there is one thing that I have had to give most to school in my life, it is my time. And on reflection, I wish the state would've used it more wisely in certain instances to broaden my understanding of civics, as well as my peers. As I believe, we would've been better off heading into private universities, trade schools, the military, and otherwise.

Civics is seldom touched upon in our American school system. We put a great deal of focus into the sciences, humanities and arts, and increasingly, into technology. While this is needed to compete with other intellectually expanding nations in order to instill a greater purpose to the learning, a sense of country needs to be encouraged. This is to ensure two components of a new American approach to civic life—integrity that the learning is for the betterment of one's own self and the pursuit of the betterment of one's community. And secondly, that an understanding of how our government works is taught. Education today has become a pseudo-capitalist tool for expanding the job market and human capital pool. Education is a means rather than an end. If we can understand that what we learn and what we do for ourselves can be used to not only better our own lives *but* the lives of our countrymen, it is then that we will be capable of having a greater sense of work aimed toward national good. Through a civic education program, we can attempt to distinguish between education and money and the correlation of the two. In order for this to effectively work, the nation needs a set of guiding values that are taught and encouraged—the ideas of work, family, community, volunteerism, charity, civility, discourse, and honor. The course would explore these concepts and ideas throughout our history through case studies of Americans who exemplify the finest aspects of our American story. Volunteerism is crucial here. While many institutions of learning require it, there is no real oversight or guideline as what constitutes as community service. These hours that many schools require should be earned through programs in conjunction with class learning whether after school, during a weekday, or on the weekends. Programs that help to foster and grow these values should be available to students through school. Taking it further, students should be required to commit a year of service over the course of their public school years to the country. To combat the sense that there is a lethargic wave and aversion to work growing in the country from a young age, we teach the value and reward of work. We must ensure that sentiments regarding school are not that of dread but are looked forward to. This requires then those students are made to understand that public school is not a right—rather, it is a great privilege that we, as a country with great wealth and resources, can provide. This is not to say that we wish to make the populace fearful that the government can take away public education, but that we attempt to end the sense of entitlement present in American society today. If we can end the sense of entitlement attached to public education, we can foster a greater appreciation for the people that make public education a reality for millions.

I mentioned earlier the idea of a national set of standards. I will touch briefly on this. A nation divided cannot move forward in its national goals, of which we have little. We have political party goals and platforms but no real national goals or works that each state is contributing to. We may start with centralizing the way in which we teach our children. While we've attempted this in recent years, too much discretion is given to the states to dictate these standards. A component of these national standards which plays into the idea of civic education is that states may choose to teach aspects of their state's history, geography, ecology, and industries. Going further, school districts may amend these to teach their children about their respective communities *in addition* to the history of the state. It is imperative that we understand where we come from, what our states produce, how they came to be, and how they operate.

The United States can continue on without these changes. But if this country wishes to remain a global power not only in its military force (which to many is the most physical measure of a nation's strength) but through education, innovation, and humanitarianism, we must encourage and work for a sense of direction and national pride. There is a reason why when we hear Frenchmen or Italians or Englishmen speak of their country, there is a certainly heightened force, a sense of pride and devotion to one's people and one's history that we seldom hear in this country. Often there is an apologetic tone taken; and while we must recognize the wrongs of our past, we should do well not to dwell and constantly bring ourselves down. The only logical way we can progress is to recognize the wrong, right the wrong, teach the wrong, and speak of it objectively—how we can learn from it? America needs to restore its sense of pride and appreciation for itself. And we can find it in our youth. They are the hope of the country. And it is our responsibility to nurture that hope and to honor the lives of that past.

Cut the Middleman: Why Current High School Education Is Irrelevant

Scott Fleisher

My high school experience was a typical one. I got up every day early in the morning, ate breakfast at school while I scrambled to complete the homework I had procrastinated on, and then I would go through my day sitting in a bunch of different classrooms, taking notes, memorizing them, and being tested on a material day in and day out. Every year had the same boring subjects: science, math, English, and history. Few electives were interesting. My entire high school career was a huge waste of time. Of course, I am not bashing subjects like English or math, but I am left with a question: If some students like these subjects, why are they not the only ones taking them? In other words, why is everyone learning the same things if everyone has different career goals and different interests?

The biggest reason it was a waste of time is simple: I not only did not care about what I was learning, but I barely remember anything. The reason I do not remember anything is also simple: none of it was relevant to what I was doing, where I was, or where I was thinking of going. There was hardly any hands-on work designed to help build skills—except for essay writing—and the work that existed never persisted past a single project. Teachers were always so focused on getting through the planned material that they always seemed focused on just getting onto the next thing.

Then they tell you that you can do well if you keep your grades up. They even tell you that you should not do extracurricular activities if you cannot keep your grades up. However, the grades we work so hard to earn in high school on subjects we do not care about do not matter in the real world. They matter only in trying to get to college, which operates in about the same manner, with a little more hands-on work. Not enough hands-on work, though, and today's employers do not care about your grades, or even if your major is relevant a lot of the time. A college degree is just an arbitrary requirement, like a high school diploma used to be that same standard. Employers care about two things: what skills you have and how much relevant work experience you have. Here is the catch. Most college graduates have neither in abundance.

I dare say that the current irrelevant high school education is the biggest root cause of this problem. I chose a high school because I understand that everybody should have some general education to foster common sense and basic knowledge. However, general education should not take up our whole lives! We learn faster the younger we are, so we should spend some of that time learning worthwhile skills and interesting, varied bodies of knowledge. Please do not make us wait until our third year in college. I would be willing to accept this kind of education through middle school, but once we get to high school, things need to change.

Here is the problem with high school today: it depends on students being obedient. Students need to sit down and listen to the teacher. They need to write notes. They need to study those notes. They have to do well on the test. They need to complete all assignments and follow all instructions exactly. That means that somebody decides what the priorities are, what goals will be pursued, what knowledge will be learned, how it will be learned when it will be learned, and how long it should take. Somewhere along the way, these people deciding everything forgot to ask all my fellow students and me what we think about that! Where does the creativity and freedom to become whom, we want to become? How can we, as students, learn skills such as goal setting when the goals are destined to us by some guy in a public office who probably never taught a day in his life? How can we, as students, figure out what we are interested in if the same subjects are always being shoved down our throats? How can we build hands-on expertise in some area if we are always forced to earn an arbitrary number grade to prove that we know useless or irrelevant knowledge?

I have an idea for that. We need to recreate the high school curriculum to allow for more variety. If students like math, English, science, or history, they should be allowed to focus on those subjects but with only students who want to learn them. If students want to devote themselves to illustration, for example, then their curriculum should be made up almost entirely of workshop courses in drawing, with a teacher who will help these students engage in deliberate practice (which is where the teacher forces the students to learn things outside their comfort zone in order to progress in their skills further). For students interested in sciences, for example, rather than just sitting in class taking notes and doing boring lab work that they will never get to do again, there should be an emphasis on research into current trends and problems so that they know how to research effectively and an emphasis on creating their lab experiments (with some guidance, but not dictatorial guidance).

There should be a way for students to learn skills they are interested in to control what they are doing and allow them the chance to get some hands-on experience that will function as a foundation for their career goals. This will allow students to go out into the world, right out of high school, to engage with these skills in more professional settings, such as internships for companies, or they can go to college to develop their skills more and gain more experiences while doing so.

We need to remember what is happening right now. Students are coming out of college with few skills and little-to-no work experiences, unable to find jobs and solve problems creatively, discovering that the system they were so obedient to has suddenly betrayed them. These are students who worked hard at what they were told to work hard at, only to find that they cannot set meaningful goals for themselves and that they have wasted eight years of their life learning nothing useful. That is typical for the younger generations, but it is not absolute. A few millennials, such as Mark Zuckerberg, were able to make something of themselves, doing things they wanted to do. The irony is that these people, for the most part, dropped out of high school or college to do so, and they turned out way better than most of us will in our lifetime. Our current education system is more likely to hold us back than push us forward. The new generations can make a lot for themselves, but many need a proper push in the right direction, and proper education is a good first step toward getting where they deserve to be.

Mental Health of the Future

Urooj Ansari

Like most students in the United States, stress is something that I have become too familiar with. Every day since kindergarten, my weeknights were spent sitting at the kitchen table completing a stack of homework. When there is a test or quiz approaching, I will spend an additional hour at the kitchen table studying. From the start, giving up playtime, free time, and sleep for schoolwork was an expectation. Starting in the third grade, I was only allowed to play on the weekends. Every night after I completed all my homework, I began to study for the standardized state tests at the end of the school year.

When I graduated elementary school and moved on into middle school, I had the standard eight-class-per-day schedule along with the increased freedom of being able to walk between classes, the small stack of homework that I had started to grow. There were days where I would have more than one quiz or test in a day. Around this time, I began to train myself to pull all-nighters to finish assignments. I was enrolled in two high school credit classes and a foreign language class in the eighth grade. Daily, we were reminded that we had three state tests, two Regents exams, and a foreign language test at the end of the school year. In the middle of all these, I also had to worry about my application to high schools and my commitments to my family and religion.

Toward the end of the eighth grade, I had severe burnout. I no longer cared about school and only continued to attend because my parents forced me to. I no longer had the motivation to put in any effort in my schoolwork and just calculated the minimum grade I would need for every class to graduate.

When I moved on to high school, my burnout followed me. The first two years of high school were extremely difficult. Unconsciously, I was taught by my peers and teachers that finishing assignments and schoolwork were something that should be at the very top of my priorities, above my physical and mental health. It was at this point that my neglected health started to catch up to me. I could not stay awake in any of my classes. I could not concentrate on anything, and I was constantly sick. It was also around this time that I started hearing rumors of students committing suicide in other schools. The reason behind their actions was the fact that they could not handle the pressure. The most frightening part was that some rumors turned out to be true stories. My biggest fear at that point was becoming one of those students.

I wanted to do well, but I could not find the effort to put in my work. My responsibilities outside of school began to grow along with the stack of assignments that I had. Since stress was the main reason most of these students decided to take their own lives, I began to look for ways to manage my stress. As I was going through various websites and blogs, I came across a concept called time management. After reading as many articles as I could find about it, I wished that I had been aware of the concept from the start. Time management takes some time to master, but with enough practice, it enables one to succeed academically while still being able to have a social life, get sleep, and take care of his/her health.

From my experience, I strongly believe that students should be taught prioritization and time management from the start. Students should be encouraged to get the recommended hours of sleep, at least forty minutes of physical activity a day, and at least three meals. I discovered this concept late in high school. If I were aware of it from the start, I might not have had severe burnout.

Time management is not a skill just for school. As I transition into college and adulthood, time management has proven to be a valuable skill. As a college student, I have to worry about my classes and my required extracurricular activities for graduate school, and my family commitments. If taught at an early age, when students reach their undergraduate years, they will have the skill perfected.

Another change that should be implemented is time off. As someone who would identify as a workaholic, I still have not learned how to do this. Overextended breaks, my peers and I are assigned almost double the amount of homework than normal. We spend our days locked up in our rooms, going through mountains of homework rather than spending time with our family and friends. Another reason why taking a break is beneficial is, so we have time to develop hobbies and other interests. Something I noticed in myself and several of my peers is that we do not have any real hobbies. Most of our time goes to academic-related work. When we do have some free time, we spend it at home, most likely binge-watching TV shows. If we were encouraged to take at least one day a week off—a day in which we have no homework or other responsibilities—we would have the time to develop hobbies.

Generally speaking, there seems to be some change in which student's health is being taken into consideration. There are some elementary schools across the country that are beginning to implement fun activities into homework assignments. Others are considering banning homework completely. Although it is being considered, we still have a long way to go. Students should not be committing suicide because they cannot handle the stress of school.

If the suggested changes are implemented, we will begin to see happier and healthier students. They will also be well-rounded and will start to do better in school. With enough effort, suicide-related to academic stress will be diminished. If action is not taken regarding this issue, the same problems we currently have will continue to affect us.

Discrimination Experienced by Students in the Education System

Nayema Laboni

Throughout US history, there have been many events of discrimination over different periods. Even though many people have taken action against the practiced discrimination, United States is believed to be one the countries with the most democracy where everyone is treated equally and has equal access to opportunity. However, even in the twenty-first century, many students face discrimination in the education system despite no rules or laws that exist to provoke discrimination or segregation.

Throughout my time as a student, I have faced discrimination myself. I came to the United States in 2009 and enrolled in Hillcrest High School as a freshman. Since then, I have experienced and seen the worst faces of the education system in the United States. When there are institutional rules to ensure better education and equal opportunities for everyone, yet the people in charge of applying or following these rules and policies and following the rules are the factors that determine the effectiveness of those rules to ensure a better education system.

The major issue is the institutionalized discrimination against the people who gain most of the local power in the education system. They are like the monarchs practicing their absolute power on students they do not like, especially on newcomers whom they think are not smart enough to fight back.

When I first came to this country, I adapted to the language and accent very fast, and people did not believe I was not born here or did not grow up here. Before I enrolled in school, I had to take tests to determine the classes I should be taking and which small learning community or SLC I should belong to. While most of the people who took the test with me went to newcomer's SLC because they needed to improve their English and needed extra help with the language, I was placed in Biztek SLC, and the person who took our exams and graded them praised how well I had written the essay. However, I had to take an ESL class as it was mandatory for a newcomer. However, I received a 95 or more each term with ease. I took the NYSESLAT on time and was exempted from ESL successfully after the first test. However, when I tried to take a regular English class, the foreign language department head tried to stop me from doing so, and he tried his best to keep me in ESL. However, I worked hard in legal ways to move out of ESL, and I was moved out of ESL to a new regular English class exactly two days before the term ended. I finished all the essays assigned for that semester in one day, and even though I did not spend much time, my new teacher gave me an 85 for my essays and complimented my organization and argument skills. However, right after she received my report card to give me in class from the previous term, which shows I was an ESL student before, her grading and communication policy changed. She used to pretend like I do not exist in the class. Whenever she communicated with me, her final point was that I do not understand anything in any circumstance; I need an extreme amount of help with classwork. When the whole class did not do her essays, she was absent many days or came in very late almost every day because, according to her, she lived very far. I studied by myself and finished her essays on time. For one essay, I was the only person to finish it and submit the essay. She still had given me a 65 for my essays and the term while others received 85 and over, even if one got a 100 in other classwork, homework, or assignment. How can one receive an 85 when he/she did not do one essay out of the two for the semester? Again I had to fight, but this time, the result was not in my favor. I loved literature since I was very young. I loved reading books, and every day after finishing my schoolwork, I used to read literature that was not in my school syllabus. I had a deep understanding of every metaphor, how they convey or relate to the theme, I had good arguments overall, and I had good skills to become a good writer. I also had good grammar because, in countries like Bangladesh, where English is the second language, the education system focuses on grammar.

Nevertheless, the endless effort to prove that a newcomer student can never be good at English did not just stop here. When I took the Regents, people who did worse than me received a better grade than me. Until I graduated, I have always had unpleasing experiences in my English classes, and my teacher never did justice for a single time. He said I probably did not write a good essay. When I showed him that my arguments and organization reflect the question perfectly, he and the person who graded my essay had to say I had sloppy handwriting. However, my other friend who had the sloppiest handwriting still had a better grade than me if the handwriting was the only issue. When my mom warned that she would go to the Education Department about it, he became scared and instantly started drinking water. However, we did not know about the legal ways we could fight the situation. I have seen people who do not know anything or do not do any work or cheat, or share works right in front of teachers get better grades just because they are favorites.

I did not just face such challenges in my English class only. Math is one of my major strengths because I naturally have good logic. I received a 99 for trigonometry in high school and similar grades in algebra. I received a 570 in the Math section of SAT with two weeks of study for all the sections, and I could not study more than two hours every day because I had school and work. I apologize if I sound like a bragger. I want to point out that I have good logic, which helps me understand what questions ask for, how to reach answers mathematically, and why we are going through effective procedures to solve problems. When I took geometry in my sophomore year in high school, my math teacher was famous for making a question a few levels higher than what we did in class. One had to think deeply to be able to reason and answer the question. Therefore, the whole class failed, including me. When I went to her reviews, she took off about 63 points for no reason. If she gave me those points, my grade would have been around 92. She suggested that I go to her after-class tutoring. After it happened a few times, I gave up and decided to accept whatever I was receiving in that class.

The discrimination did not just happen in classes. They happened for extracurricular activities as well. I wanted to perform in an international dance festival for school, and I was denied the opportunity while someone else with less knowledge and skills replaced me. I could provide my videos—and if her videos exist, then hers—to provide a way of comparison. This happened only because she was a favorite student of the person taking auditions. People were disappointed, and they criticized the only solo dance performance. Later on, I wanted to run for any of the positions available for the Bengali Club of my school. Its purpose was to unite and celebrate the Bengali holidays.

Even though I had performed in several TV and stage shows and I have good knowledge about the culture, the club's supervisor did not want me to run for the positions and wanted her favorite students to hold the positions. He was extremely disrespectful as he told me I was not a good fit for the position, but he did not explain the qualities I lacked that were necessary for the positions. I explained to him that I had a better understanding of the culture and shows; therefore, I could help them plan shows. However, he did not want to allow me to run for election. When I was determined to do it, he spread negative comments about me to people, such as I was crazy. I am not sure if he meant I had a mental illness, which my doctor at that time never sensed or doubted. I was not allowed to run for the positions during the election. So I decided to start my own Bengali Cultural Club with my best friends, and we had someone that agreed to become our supervisor. With the supervisor and my friends' support, I held at least six shows a year; all those shows had better performers chosen by my friends and me. We had better plans, decorations and organizations, better parties, and more people enjoying and asking for more parties even after I graduated. I worked hard to plan, organize, and perform at those parties.

Discrimination is not the only negative experience I had in high school. I also had been physically attacked by students in front of teachers, and teachers did nothing. While getting ready in the gym for performance, some girls gathered and pushed me against lockers. My peers saw it happening and ran away with fear. My gym teacher was right next to us, but instead of taking any action about it, she told me to shake my hands with them. Around the same time, one of my peers from my DNA biotechnology class hit me on the back of my head and then ran to the hallway, walking around the hallways for the rest of the period cursing at me right after I asked something she had supplies for provided by the teacher for a class project. I had asked for the supplies from her respectfully. When all these were happening, our teacher just watched as she seemed scared, and she was hiding her face behind the attendance folder. I tried to leave class to go to the guidance counselor after asking permission from the teacher. In the hallway, the deans stopped me and yelled at me until I went back to the classroom, but these same people could not stop my peer from running around the hallway cursing at me.

I have had really bad experiences overall, which were strong enough to negatively impact my confidence, determination, setting, and goals, even though I tried my best to fight all the obstacles I faced in high school to move upward. For example, after these experiences, I have decided to study computer science, where grading is not subjective, but more concrete based on math or coding. Since this field is more concentrated on immigrants, I have had better experiences in this field and decided to stay away from any writing-intensive major. There will always be some form of obstacle in many sectors of life, but I hope no other students that are newcomers face obstacles to the extreme I have.

Nevertheless, discrimination can be controlled or, if

people tried hard, can be eliminated. To prevent discrimination faced by students, there should be more rules and regulations to ensure equality among students. Also, whether the rules and regulations are being enforced properly should be monitored. Additionally, the government should enact laws to punish whenever an educator or people in the education system practice discrimination. These laws should be enforced as well. There should be more ways to reach students and their parents about what a student's right is as a student and the legal procedures a student or parent could follow if they face discrimination based on the case. In addition to these, the information could be mailed to student's house, create websites with the information, or an official from the school can call the parents or leave a message about the rights and rules, or let them know of the website, as well as send e-mails to parents.

If the discrimination in the US education system is not being suppressed, the United States will lose many talents who could contribute to the country's overall development due to lack of opportunity or if the potential students quit due to the experiences they had. The solutions I have proposed could suppress the discrimination in the education system and help many students going through psychological trauma, such as low self-esteem, depression, or suicide due to the discrimination they face in school. The solutions will also help the country lose some potential students who might be unambitious or quit pursuing their dreams due to the discrimination they have faced.

Freedom to Teach

Joy Lam

The US education has changed little throughout the years. While still following the same routine for testing how well students can understand concepts and formulas, it has altered the purpose of learning. How teachers teach students is applied to the average students, given they have no issue understanding the information and have no unknown variables that impede them from learning a subject. I understand the issue with catering to each student as it takes time and extra planning; however, it does not sound pleasing when we are teaching students to pass the class or learning. I propose that we change how teachers teach students. Instead of following a rigorous template of what to teach, they should teach the basics to students and then teach what the students prefer and what the teachers prefer. A teacher should cater to the class's needs and to what students want to learn after the basics. Where is the passion to teach? Where is the passion for learning?

From pre-K to twelfth grade, I have undergone the bulk of my life in the US education system in New York City, which means tests and grades rule your academic life. When statewide exams became a mandatory thing, teachers were rushed to teach as much as possible, catering their lesson plans around Regents exams and making sure we pass. There was little time to understand the material, let alone learn new topics. It was a sink or swim fiasco. Arriving in college, I have encountered professors who have the flexibility to teach what they want, and some professors were even passionate about what they were teaching despite having to follow a course outline given to them by their department! There was some freedom, as long as they taught what they must teach.

Nonetheless, the most exciting times would be learning outside topics, whether about our professor's research or the class interest. I believe a teacher should be the main factor to influence their students to be motivated and passionate about what they are learning. Being a computer science major, I must have a supportive and motivated community of peers and teachers to push me forward, and I realized how much impact teachers can make for students to find something they are passionate about learning. However, with the strict system of exams and what must be taught, the beauty in learning and freedom to learn and teach are taken away.

I suggest that there be more freedom for teachers to teach. That means taking away the state exams and trusting the teachers to give the appropriate grade to their students. Students should be trusted to make their own decisions. If they refuse to learn, then the teacher must decide what to do. It is the teachers' job to teach and the student's job to learn. Students should not be looked at as young and naive but pushed to be adults and make their own decisions. If they decide not to learn, then they should know the consequences. Teach students something the teacher is interested in once in a while, while related to the subject. Teach students life skills, like how to file your taxes or social skills. Things that, surprisingly, people might have problems overcoming.

There is no right way to teach, as there are many different kinds of students. However, teachers should not give up on students because they refuse to learn. Teachers should challenge themselves and their students. Challenge them to be better and to want to learn. The education system is not a factory spitting out qualified students. The education system should be a place for students to learn and be their human beings; it is a choice.

So far, the US education system will continue down its track to produce well-rounded students. As for the future, the board of education will most likely administer other programs, which are supposed to unify what is being taught to all students statewide. Of course, nothing much will change since we have been following a century-plus long system. It will be pretty difficult to change all those around. However, my given proposal to allow teachers the freedom to teach will most likely segregate schools, and it will not be easy to manage realistically. There will be some teachers who can adapt and help their students blossom, but many will fail. This is also due to where those teachers learn to teach and how their education and experience can help them foster with this given freedom. Of course, ideally, I would hope that students be more passionate about learning and be adults. I would hope the education system would be more "human" in a sense where passion, understanding, and learning thrive.

Institutionalize Mandated Diversity

Yelena Dzhanova

At least in New York State, a public school education attracts wealthier parents by flaunting its Gifted & Talented accelerated programs. The appeal to sending a child to public school rests in the guarantee that a child would be on the receiving end of an eye-catching combination of the best possible and most economically feasible education. Upon entering elementary school, parents of prospective pupils may opt for their children to take an exam that determines their mental aptitude. If these students score in the top percentile, they move on to the Gifted & Talented program. The program also maintains a hardcore waitlist, ready for new children, should accept students decline the offer or fail out.

These programs are mostly filled with students whose parents are more affluent when it comes to economic matters. Demographically and statistically, the majority of these parents happen to be white. Closely following in the program's population are Asian parents. Black, Hispanic and Latino, and brown parents do not share these statistics. Therefore, as beneficial as the program appears to be, its selected participants nevertheless will always remain deprived of developing a truly global and realistic human connection and interaction. Few cultures and countries represented that not the best education that can be taken away is purely a whitewashed and highly Westernized one. The Gifted & Talented program students reflect nothing but their own cultures, and this can only and at best permit learning in the short term. Diversity in the classroom increases global perspective and encourages students, especially younger students, to think of the world as shared rather than solely their own. This has the remarkable potential to inspire them to work together and instill fearlessness to tackle major issues when working in conjunction peacefully.

The value to increasing diversity within classrooms, in the general sense, is the fact that it often accompanies desirable traits such as openness, tolerance, respect, curiosity, and understanding. Breaking barriers are only possible during youth—the age of innocence. If students go into the Gifted & Talented program surrounded by mostly white and Asian kids, it will give them the predisposition to attach certain stereotypes and traits to themselves that they may put on reserve for other underrepresented groups of people.

Children who go into a classroom and see all sorts of races and ethnicities are more likely to avoid labeling and generalizing large groups of people into pools of certain characteristics. These students would be more inclined to think of their classroom as a vast world where everyone is on the same page. Think of a classroom whose greatest feature is its lack of diversity as an isolated region of the world, unreachable to other countries. To contrast, think of a classroom whose walls are teeming with diverse faces as a central nation surrounded by oceans and waterways, and neighboring lands. The latter would attract more development and spread of knowledge. On the other hand, the former would likely collapse due to a lack of resources and shared knowledge.

Humans work better as a team. Everyone brings something different that can be used to solve a problem or expand on successful endeavors. Although it is not quite a segregated effort in these classes—and to imply so would be a little bewildering—it is an effort that is inappropriately and negligently separating.

Colleges and universities also recognize the issue of a strong lack of diversity on their campuses. This is, in part, why affirmative action has been instilled within many university admissions systems. This system is in place because it is an effort to make some reparations for white oppressors' issues caused to arise.

American journalist and cultural critic Ta-Nehisi Coates explained in his essay "A Case for Reparations" (which was published in *The Atlantic*) that although slavery does not legally exist anymore, historical events such as slavery have caused a huge imbalance in the opportunities black people can pursue and achieve. Because of the negative relations and tensions between white and black people, particularly when slavery was legal, white people came out more prosperous centuries later. Black people, on the other hand, suffered. They suffered so much that the effects can be examined at large today. This carries out in thought and media consumption and alters the way human beings interact with one another.

Colleges, however, have taken a step toward remedying these stark injustices. Other selective institutions and programs worldwide, much like New York's Gifted & Talented, have not attempted to level out the disparities, even though countless benefits exist to mandating educational diversity.

My own story is not dissimilar. I was placed into the Gifted & Talented program in elementary school and stayed in it until I got to middle school, at which point, I was given a chance to be in an honors class. I went on to one of the best high schools in the country and, upon graduation, to one of the best colleges in the country. After high school, I was shocked that I seemed to be underrepresented in my college's demographics. It seemed like there were more people of color than white people. I only realized I had lived in a bubble for the entirety of my childhood upon entering college and starting a new chapter as an adult. I feel as though I would have benefitted from more diversity in each of my settings, simply because while I have always understood that racism was morally wrong and culture should be celebrated, I got the impression that I could have been more of an open person. Perhaps it is because of the lack of diversity I feel as though I have faced during my schooling, or perhaps it is the overexposure to social justice and politics that I have acquired over the years on my own. However, something makes me feel like I have to make sure there is no distinction between my peers or me. I speculate that if I had grown up in an environment where I was more accustomed to people of different skin colors and ethnicities outside of my own, I would not feel this way. Maybe that is not necessarily the truth, but there is value in what I am feeling. I feel a distinction, and I make every effort to cover it up, but maybe I never should have felt this way.

It is precisely this that drives me to say that diversity must be institutionally implemented, even in programs for children as young as kindergarteners. If greater diversity in a classroom setting is not implemented, it will suffice to say that children would grow up in something akin to a bubble, familiar to only what the boundaries of that bubble contain. Children, in turn, would grow up more prone to shock and bigotry as they age. Our world can only truly coexist when we work as a team of one race, rather than split up by mere differences that have no bearing on our cohesiveness. We must allow ourselves to pop any existing bubbles and broaden our horizons.

Students must see that everyone has equal opportunities and that race or ethnicity, or class does not grant privilege or power of any sort. The only solutions are to either mandate diversity within all classroom settings or eliminate the elite programs and systems by mixing all students and treating them individually.

Student's Education Institution Transition

Maruf Hossain

A student's transition from a school to another school can most definitely be frustrating and struggling. When you walk into a new learning environment, you are faced with new administrations, new faces, and for a college, almost on your own where you are required to figure things out on your own. The struggling transition was no different for me as well. I faced a confusing and misinformed transition from my community college to my senior college. The transition, as smooth as it seemed, turned out to be a nightmare personally for me.

In 2013, I transitioned from City University of New York's (CUNY) Borough of Manhattan Community College (BMCC) to Hunter College. As I was making my transition, I remembered clearly that I just got done with my orientation at Hunter College. I was told of all the types of classes I needed to take. To hear that, as a psychology major and just a student of the college, I had about four or five different classes I had to take. Hearing that was not intimidating; I already had done that multiple times at BMCC. However, when I went to register for classes, I saw that I could not register for my psychology course. So I went to my major's department, trying to figure all this out, and they saw I took statistics at BMCC. However, I was told I had to retake statistics because I did not pass the course with a C or better—I had passed with a D.

Just hearing that gave me frightening and nerve-racking thoughts of my past about how difficult statistics was at BMCC, and that to not keep my grade up toward the end of the class when I took it the first time around. I was in a mindset of wanting to escape statistics and not take it ever again because of my experience. Therefore, I asked my adviser, "What are alternatives to statistics for me to get to take statistical methods in psychology course?" I was told I could take precalculus as the alternative if I did not want to take statistics again. Therefore, I went on to try to register for precalculus. However, I was still not able to register for that. That was when I had to become my assertive self, turned it up a notch, and started running around to find the core of the problem. I went from office to office, and it landed me right into the testing office.

In the testing office, I told them the problem I was facing, and they went on to check my records from BMCC. They told me that I had to take a pre-101 workshop, which meant a remedial course. From there, I went on to the math learning center to register for the pre-101 workshop. I decided then since I was so behind in my studies in terms of the number of classes I had to take and since I would have had to take an unbalanced course load between hard and easy courses that I only would take the workshop and nothing else because, with the choices I had for classes, I would have set myself up for failure. A semester passed by, and I was just a few days away from taking the final exam of the workshop. From there, I was one day given a practice exam of the type of test I had to take toward the end of the semester for me to move on to a credit-bearing course.

However, when I looked at the practice exam, it looked quite familiar to me. Then I asked about the exam, and to my shock, I found out it was the CUNY placement exam—the same exam I did not pass at BMCC with a grade satisfying enough for Hunter. I was in shock, and I was freaking out. I did not want to do anything. My tutor saw that I was unaware of the workshop the learning center put me in. Then I went to the director. I told the director my entire story, and she realized I was completely misinformed of my status with math by the testing center. Then she gave me hope of relief and told me that if I could pass the final exam with a high grade, she would put me directly into Math 101, which was algebra for college students. Luckily, I passed the CUNY placement exam with a grade in the high 90s. It was after that I finally started Hunter in fall 2014.

I was not able to become a student for spring 2014 because I had to reapply to Hunter College since I had not taken any credit-bearing course in fall 2013—I was focusing on the workshop and trying not to overwhelm myself with other courses that did not balance out between easy and hard courses. Therefore, it was not until fall 2014 where I was a full-time student for the first time at Hunter College, and I was taking algebra for college students like I was originally told to. Other complications played out, like getting no credit for the algebra class because math was the worst subject in school throughout my lifetime. That made me retake statistics eventually and repeat the course. Luckily, Hunter had a much better format of teaching statistics that made me pass statistics in spring 2015 with an average grade, so I could finally start taking my psychology course. It was a time-consuming one-and-a-half-year-long process until I was able to see a psychology course again in the summer of 2015.

The issue described in something like I have experienced in particular is highly unheard of; however, the change required here is a better way to inform students of their college education and guide them properly. This can be categorized as issues students face with the administration. Students face many forms of administrative issues and being misinformed is not tolerable by students. There should be a better process of helping first-time college and transfer students transition into college rather than just making them run around independently trying to figure things out for themselves. Yes, we understand, as college students, we are not kids, and we do not need someone to hold our hands as adults. However, I suggest giving first-time college and transfer students at least a mentor of their studying field, a college ambassador, or college student leaders for their first year at the new institution. If incoming first-year students of a college or transfer students are to be paired up with someone of their field of study or an upperclassman, they will be more likely to start college off on the right path and be much more successful the first year as college students.

This idea of having a mentor is not simply for someone to tell an incoming freshman or transfer what to do but for someone to be actively involved in seeing where the student is with his/her education and what the next step is. The student himself should be able to take care of his/her duties as a student in terms of doing any administrative work required and going to offices to take care of it. However, in things like being sure of the education status, what classes to take so it is properly balanced, and administrative issues a student may be facing that he is unfamiliar with. This mentor can also teach the student how to go about his/her first year in college, with the academic and student life in the college. The mentor should be available at the student's disposal for any extraneous issues and the transitioning process.

The mentor will play a pivotal role in the student's life for the first year to properly guide the student to do his/her best to have a better academic outcome after the first year. If a college student messes up his/her first year in college, especially without a proper foundation and understanding of the college expectations and studying methods, it cannot be easy to get back on track to raise his/her GPA back up and maintain it. The mentor is not there to baby the student but can properly transition to a new college and have a good first-year experience.

The administration also plays an important role in all of this. The administration should be trained to tackle unusual problems and properly inform students of what to do or where to go. I feel all the necessary information should be available to each administrative office, and they should have a good grasp and understanding of the information on their computer screen. I understand all offices have a specific responsibility and information to give students, but they should have information to look up all forms of their records and plan to guide students to the appropriate office or individual. No student should be given the runaround by administering their college with a lack of information or the wrong information. When students walk into an office, they expect to be properly informed. Most of the time, they will know where to go in the first place for student's common problems. However, let us say something out of the ordinary does come up—where do you expect the students to go?

They are doing their part of being go-getters, but that

is not all that is required. This has two parts in the play. The students have to do their part of being go-getters and fulfilling their responsibilities as students and taking care of whatever they need to take care of. However, the second part is for the administration. The administration should take their time to understand what problem the student is facing properly. They should look at everything required to fix the issue, especially if the student is in the right office already. The administration should inform the students of their status, not just by what they need to move on to the next step but, if needed, where the students are with their status or issue, they are facing.

Student's future-facing administrative problems may never end; however, these issues that trouble students, especially with the most common problems, should be tackled by the US education system and the school administration. With the proposed changes of having a mentor for a freshman and transfer student and administration being more diligent and taking their time to help out these students, we can advance in our administrative offices of colleges. There have to be advances and out-of-box thinking to those answers and fix college student's problems regarding the administration. Many of these issues can be time-consuming, so diligence and having proper answers in the administrative offices is something students hope for. Without these changes, we are stuck in a stale system and with an administrative staff that is not properly trained or retraining.

Administrative issues are a leading issue that students in college become frustrated with and consume their time. Whether it be figuring out what college courses to take or where to go, there is always something students face within their college that has to do with the administrative offices. Having a mentor is highly beneficial for newcomers and transfer students. It does not leave students up in the air where they feel lost and unsure of what to do. Regardless of anything, college students have to do their part and make an effort to take care of any issue they are facing. A mentor and a well-trained administration are something students would hope for and agree to.

Contributors

Corrina Blau—Corrina Blau is the writer of "Education's Purpose." She is a graduate of Hunter College in the City University of New York (CUNY) and was a sophomore at the time she wrote her story. She planned to major in sociology and hopes to dedicate her career to fighting poverty in New York City.

Raimondo Graziano—Raimondo Graziano is the writer of "Diversified Approach to American Education and Civics in Education." He was attending Hunter College and was undeclared at the time he wrote his story but wished to pursue a major in economics and a minor in public policy. Graziano, for much of his high school years, has been active on the school paper and an active member of the 105th Precinct Community Board, working to address public issues in the district, representing the Rockaway and Broad Channel. Graziano hopes to continue a life in public service, operating a small theatre company out of Queens, New York, with a hope that, one day, educational theatre programs can be provided to school children in Queens and eventually the Greater New York area.

Scott Fleisher—Scott Fleisher is the writer of "Cut the Middleman: Why Current High School Education Is Irrelevant." He was an undergraduate student at Hunter College majoring in media studies. Fleisher's been focused on learning about the education system and how the media works, bringing these pieces together to understand the modern student. Independently for a little over a year, he was still undecided on how he will proceed. Nevertheless, he spends his time studying the interplay of media and education in the age of information and aims to work toward education reform in the future.

Urooj Ansari—Urooj Ansari is the writer of "Mental Health of the Future." At the time she wrote her story, she was a student at Hunter College. She planned on going to graduate school in the future, focusing on the sciences. She was also a member of the Muslim Student Association (MSA) at Hunter and an intern at a startup.

Nayema Laboni—Nayema Laboni is the writer of "Discrimination Experienced by Students in the Education System." She was a student at Hunter College, majoring in computer science with a minor in political science. She graduated from Hillcrest High School with an honors Regents diploma from Pre-Med SLC. Laboni has received a certificate from Congressman Daniel Dromm for contributing to Bengali culture and poor women in need in Bangladesh and America. She hoped to use her computer science knowledge and skills to influence the policies of United States to lessen discrimination in as many different fields as possible.

Joy Lam—Joy Lam is the writer of "Freedom to Teach." She was a student at Hunter College, studying computer science. She planned to be a consultant in the tech community or a software developer. Being a part of the education system for most of her life, she stresses the importance in being curious and in having a thirst of knowledge and learning.

Yelena Dzhanova—Yelena Dzhanova is the writer of "Institutionalize Mandated Diversity." She was a sophomore attending Baruch College in CUNY at the time she wrote her story. She has served as a writer, editor, and contributor to many community publications. Dzhanova is politically active in that she has campaigned on behalf of local politicians, fought to raise the minimum wage, and worked on getting a bill passed to eliminate discrimination against people who identify with the LGBT community. She hoped to become an editor for one of her favorite magazines, *Time* or *The Atlantic*.

Bibliography

Chapter 1

1. Alcocer, Paulina, NEA Education Policy, and Practice Intern, "History of Standardized Testing in the United States," 2002, accessed November 24, 2016, http://www.nea.org/home/66139.htm.

2. American College Testing Program, "Annual Report 2015." 2015, accessed November 24, 2016, http://www.act.org/content/dam/act/unsecured/documents/AnnualReport2015.pdf.

3. Concepts, Liberty. 2016, "Portfolio Definition," *The Glossary of Education Reform*, http://edglossary.org/portfolio/.

4. Partnership, Great Schools and Liberty Concepts, "Portfolio Definition," May 15, 2013, accessed November 24, 2016, http://edglossary.org/portfolio/.

5. Stetc..her, Brian, "Performance Assessment in an Era of Standards-Based Educational Accountability," 2010, accessed November 24, 2016, https://scale.stanford.edu/system/files/performance-assessment-era-standards-based-educational-accountability.pdf.

6. US Congress, Office of Technology Assessment, "Testing in American Schools: Asking the Right Question," February 1992, accessed November 24, 2016, https://www.princeton.edu/~ota/disk1/1992/9236/9236.PDF.

Chapter 2

7. The Bully Project, "The BULLY Project," accessed November 26, 2016, http://www.thebullyproject.com/.

8. Do Something.org, "11 Facts about Bullying," accessed November 25, 2016, https://www.dosomething.org/us/facts/11-facts-about-bullying.

9. Office for Civil Rights, "US Department of Education," May 4, 2015, accessed November 29, 2016, http://www2.ed.gov/about/offices/list/ocr/index.html.

10. ———, "US Department of Education," July 21, 2016, accessed November 29, 2016, http://www2.ed.gov/about/offices/list/ocr/docs/howto.html.

11. Sacirby, Omar, "Muslim Teens Push Back Against 9/11 Bullying," *Huffington Post* (The Huffington Post), September 8, 2011, http://www.huffingtonpost.com/2011/09/07/bullying-muslim-teens-push-back_n_952947.html.

12. Stand for the Silent, "End Bullying with Stand for the Silent," 2010, accessed November 26, 2016, http://www.standforthesilent.org/.

13. US Department of Health & Human Services, "Considerations for Specific Groups," March 8, 2012, accessed November 25, 2016, https://www.stopbullying.gov/at-risk/groups/.

14. US Department of Health and Human Services, "Federal Laws," March 8, 2012, accessed November 25, 2016, https://www.stopbullying.gov/laws/federal/index.html.

15. The United States Department of Justice, "Types of Educational Opportunities Discrimination," August 7, 2015, accessed November 26, 2016, https://www.justice.gov/crt/types-educational-opportunities-discrimination.

16. World Wrestling Entertainment (WWE), "Be a STAR," accessed November 26, 2016, https://community.wwe.com/diversity/programs/be-star.

Chapter 3

17. National Education Association, *Parent, Family, Community Involvement in Education. PB11 ParentInvolvement08*, Washington, DC: National Education Association, 2008, http://www.nea.org/assets/docs/PB11_ParentInvolvement08.pdf.

18. Ferguson, HB, S Bovaird, and MP Mueller, "The Impact of Poverty on Educational Outcomes for Children," *"Paediatr Child Health"* 12, no. 8 (October 1, 2007), accessed December 3, 2016, https://www.ncbi.nlm.nih.gov/pmc/articles/PMC2528798/.

19. Foundation, The Heritage, "Family Structure and Children's Education," 2016, accessed December 3, 2016, http://www.familyfacts.org/briefs/35/family-structure-and-childrens-education.

20. Mgbemere, Bianca and Rachel Telles, "Types of Parenting Styles and How to Identify Yours," December 10, 2013, accessed December 3, 2016, https://my.vanderbilt.edu/developmentalpsychologyblog/2013/12/types-of-parenting-styles-and-how-to-identify-yours/.

Chapter 4

21. American Accreditation Healthcare Commission, "Mathematics Disorder," December 2, 2016, accessed December 12, 2016, https://medlineplus.gov/ency/article/001534.htm.

22. Division, Civil Rights, "2010 ADA Regulations," March 1, 2013, accessed December 9, 2016, https://www.ada.gov/2010_regs.htm.

23. LaCombe, Susan, "Left and Right Brain Function," 2006, accessed December 11, 2016, http://www.myshrink.com/left-right-brain-function.php.

24. Learning Disabilities Association of America, "Types of Learning Disabilities," 2016, accessed December 9, 2016, https://ldaamerica.org/types-of-learning-disabilities/.

25. The United States Department of Justice, "Types of Educational Opportunities Discrimination," August 7, 2015, accessed December 9, 2016, https://www.justice.gov/crt/types-educational-opportunities-discrimination.

26. Lang, Susan S, "Learning a Second Language Is Good Childhood Mind Medicine, Studies Find," December 12, 2016, accessed December 12, 2016, https://www.news.cornell.edu/stories/2009/05/learning-second-language-good-childhood-mind-medicine.

27. The Urban Child Institute, "Language and Literacy," 2016, accessed December 12, 2016, http://www.urbanchildinstitute.org/why-0-3/language-and-literacy.

Chapter 5

28. Department for Professional Employees, "School Administrators: An Occupational Overview," 2001, accessed December 16, 2016, http://dpeaflcio.org/programs-publications/issue-fact-sheets/school-administrators-an-occupational-overview/.

29. Hollowell, Karen, "Problems in Educational Administration," September 24, 2015, accessed December 16, 2016, http://www.ehow.com/about_5471370_problems-educational-administration.html.

30. Kennedy, Mike, "Top Ten: Issues Impacting School Administrators," January 1, 2001, accessed December 16, 2016, http://asumag.com/mag/university_top_ten_issues.

Chapter 6

31. Camera, Lauren, "Federal Education Funding: Where Does the Money Go?" January 14, 2016, accessed December 31, 2016, http://www.usnews.com/news/blogs/data-mine/2016/01/14/federal-education-funding-where-does-the-money-go.

32. Educational Finance Branch, *Public Education Finances: 2014*, *Public Education Finances: 2014*, US Government Printing Office, Washington, DC: US Census Bureau, 2016, http://census.gov/content/dam/Census/library/publications/2016/econ/g14-aspef.pdf.

33. National Association for College Admission Counseling, "What's the Price Tag for a College Education?" 2016, accessed December 31, 2016, http://www.

collegedata.com/cs/content/content_payarticle_tmpl.jhtml?articleId=10064.

34. National Center for Education Statistics, "Fast Facts," 2016, accessed December 31, 2016, https://nces.ed.gov/fastfacts/display.asp?id=76.

35. "What's the Price Tag for a College Education?" Collegedata, 2016, accessed December 31, 2016, http://www.collegedata.com/cs/content/content_payarticle_tmpl.jhtml?articleId=10064.

36. PLC, Pearson, "The Learning Curve," 2016, accessed December 31, 2016, http://thelearningcurve.pearson.com/index/index-ranking.

37. Santiago, Deborah, "Should College Be Free?" *The Opinion Pages*, January 20, 2016, http://www.nytimes.com/roomfordebate/2016/01/20/should-college-be-free/the-problem-is-that-free-college-isnt-free.

38. US Department of Education, *Fact Sheet-US Department of Education. Funding Highlights*. n.p.: US Department of Education, 2015, https://www2.ed.gov/about/overview/budget/budget16/budget-factsheet.pdf.

39. "Wise-Working in Support of Education," Wise, 2006, accessed December 31, 2016, http://www.wise-ny.org/programs.htm

Chapter 8

40. College Board, "Students Speak: What College Social Life Is Really Like," 2017, accessed January 13, 2017, https://bigfuture.collegeboard.org/find-colleges/campus-life/students-speak-what-college-social-life-is-really-like.

41. Pranabudi, Indira, "What to Know About the US College Experience Before Applying," 2014, accessed January 13, 2017, http://www.usnews.com/education/blogs/international-student-counsel/2014/09/09/what-to-know-about-the-us-college-experience-before-applying.

42. Staff, CC, "The First Year College Experience," November 30, 1999, accessed January 13, 2017, http://www.collegeconfidential.com/first-year/.

Author's Biography

Maruf Hossain has a Master of Arts in Psychology from Pace University in New York City, focusing on developmental psychology and a research career. He hopes to finish his education by going for a Ph.D. in developmental psychology in the future. Maruf was an education advocate throughout his undergraduate in the Borough of Manhattan Community College (BMCC) and Hunter College under the City University of New York (CUNY). As an education advocate, he contributed his time in CUNY as a student, education advocate, and being part of a student-led organization to bring about change in the system but more specifically in his college programs, Percy Ellis Sutton Search for Education Elevation and Knowledge (SEEK) and the College Discovery Program. One of his biggest achievements was serving as a vice-chair to his organization, United Leaders of CUNY, a student-run organization led and ran by the SEEK and College Discovery Program students. During Maruf's tenure as an education advocate, his biggest accomplishment was being quoted by the Professional Staff Congress in CUNY (PSC- CUNY) in their February 2013 article "Tough Going for Pathways: Fall 2013 Implementation May Be Hard to Reach" by Peter Hogness. By profession, Maruf is a developmental psychology researcher, starting his career in the summer of 2017. He is looking to expand in his field of study by looking for jobs that cater to special needs children, typical children, and families within New York City. He hopes to write other books on the education system, topics on developmental psychology in particular with mental health, family, parenting skills, awareness of children and young adult's mental health issues to bring awareness on various issues and educate the public. Maruf is the CEO and founder of the Academy for Career and Education Development (Facebook/Twitter: @ACEDInstitute), in which he advises, teaches, and motivates student's 11th grade and up and first-time professionals in focusing on their academics and how to go about choosing a career that is fulfilling. Currently, the company has an active Facebook and Twitter social media account of the company, and he hopes to relaunch the company website in the future. Many who know him would describe him as a wounded warrior who has been motivated by life experiences to give back to the future generations. Aside from his career, he hopes to find opportunities to work with children, families, and special needs children in NYC and wherever his life takes him. He hopes to work and find opportunities to combine the education field and developmental psychology to give back to kids and families in his profession.

www.ingramcontent.com/pod-product-compliance
Ingram Content Group UK Ltd.
Pitfield, Milton Keynes, MK11 3LW, UK
UKHW041953230426
12048UKWH00008B/307